BE A PRO

ISBN: 978-19-5-315360-9

Published by

If you are interested in publishing through Lifestyle Entrepreneurs Press, write to: *Publishing@LifestyleEntrepreneursPress.com*

Publications or foreign rights acquisition of our catalog books.
Learn More: *www.LifestyleEntrepreneursPress.com*

Printed in the USA

BE A PRO

YOUR BLUEPRINT TO PROFESSIONAL LEVEL ACHIEVEMENT

JIMMY FARRIS

Editorial Project Management: Karen Rowe, *www.karenrowe.com*

To My Parents, Bob and Sharon.

I could never express how grateful I am to the both of you. I hope I've made you proud. I love you.

"If you want things to get better, you have to get better."
— Jim Rohn

CONTENTS

CONTENTS

INTRODUCTION

This book is not your typical personal development, self-help, or business book. It's not full of feel-good stories or embellished tales about my feats as an athlete. I'm not going to cite multiple case studies, surveys, or examples of how others have turned their personal lives or businesses around using the latest cutting-edge success hacks. You won't find the latest discoveries in psychology or neuroscience in the following pages. I highly value contributions from those fields of study, but that's not the approach I'm going to use in this book. This book is simply about getting better and being your best.

Notice I didn't say *the* best, but *your* best.

What makes *me* an authority on being your best? Well, when I was ten years old, I set a goal to play in the NFL. But, unlike a lot of ten year olds, I actually did it.

I still have the piece of paper on which that goal was written. I remember it like it was yesterday. On the first day of fifth grade, my teacher, Mr. Bruce, handed out a little "packet" to the class. It was titled *All About Me* and was intended to help him learn more about each of his students and help us get to know the other kids in class. The packet included questions about our favorite foods, movies, TV shows, songs, and so on. It also asked us about our favorite sport (mine was football), our secret wish (mine was to play pro football), and finally, our goal in life (to which I answered, to play pro football).

Thirteen years later, I realized that dream. I spent a total of six years in the NFL and was lucky enough to play for some of the best teams in the league. I even won a Super Bowl with the Patriots my rookie year. The lessons I learned on that journey—along with everything I know about getting better and being your best—are in this book. In little over a decade since I officially retired from the NFL, I have been fortunate to coach and train many world-class professionals across multiple industries, including CEOs, business owners, and health and fitness professionals, on the mindset tools, habits, and principles world-class athletes use to achieve greatness and stay at the top of their game consistently.

Now, let me level with you. I was never the best football player in the world. I was an average-size, average-speed, moderately physically gifted athlete who was able to make it to the highest level of professional football, the NFL, because I did the simple, basic things at an extraordinarily high level. There was not one defining action that made it all happen. No singular event that made the difference. Rather, it was small, simple, daily habits and actions, done repeatedly, for years, that took me from setting the goal to realizing it.

I became the best I could be, and in the pages that follow, I'm going to tell you how I did it. I'm going to give you a blueprint you can follow to take control of your results, get better in any area of your personal or professional life, and live a life full of significance, happiness, and fulfillment.

One of my coaches used to say, "You're either getting better or you're getting worse. There is no staying the same." My NFL career was made possible because I consistently chose to get better. My hope is that this book will inspire you to make the same choice I did.

I believe that anyone can get better at anything and become the best version of themselves. The title of this book, **Be a Pro**, is a simple phrase that means be your best—bring your A-game when and where it matters. It means do whatever it takes to get the job done, reach new heights, and create the best version of yourself by becoming more **Prepared**, **Reliable**, and **Obsessed**. Attaining your absolute best will require you to get better. And getting better is a continuous, never-ending process.

As an athlete, every time I thought I had played my best game or turned in my best performance, my first thought was, *Can I be even better?* The answer was always, *Yes!* The same is true for you.

No matter where you are right now in the key areas of your life—health, relationships, career, finances, personal development, or any other areas of life you value—**you can get better**. And by getting better, you can be, do, and have more of the things you want in life. But getting better requires putting in the effort. You must develop the necessary habits, make the sacrifices required, and do the work.

You want to be a millionaire? You can do it. Do you want an amazing relationship? You can have that, too. Do you want a great career, your dream life—success, happiness, and fulfillment? From material possessions to great relationships, health, and ultimate happiness and fulfillment, you can have it all! But in order for *things* to get better, *you* have to get better first. The best, ideal version of yourself exists, and you *can* become that person.

You can create the life you want, accomplish your goals, and live out your dreams. In the following pages, I plan to prove that to you. If you don't believe me, you have two choices: You can stop reading right now and continue on your current path, leaving your growth and success up to chance. Or you can suspend your disbelief and allow me the opportunity to change your mind.

And let me be clear; there is no one *right* way to achieve a goal or realize a dream. This book simply describes the best way that I know—a blueprint I believe can be effective regardless of where you are starting or where you are trying to go.

A Few Disclaimers

Before we dive into the meat of this book, I need to get a few important disclaimers out of the way.

First of all, this is going to take some *work*. Decades of personal experience working with super-high performers across multiple industries have confirmed in my mind the fact that if you want to be your absolute best at anything, you can do it, but there are no shortcuts, hacks, silver bullets, or fairy dust, like many in the self-help and personal-development industry would have you believe. You have to **work for it, plan for it, and be obsessive about attaining it**.

You must be willing to do what it takes. Big things and small things alike. Things you want to do and things you really *don't* want to do. In this book are the tools, habits, and principles needed to make that possible. But it requires *action*.

All of my life, I've heard the phrase "knowledge is power." I call bullshit on that. **Knowledge is potential, not power**. Because, when it comes right down to it, most people know what to do, but they don't do what they know. If you don't execute on what you know, your knowledge is useless.

Simply put, you have to be intentional about your growth. You can't leave these things to chance. You can't hope that it will just *happen.* It takes consistent, dedicated action, with full commitment to your desired outcome. One foot in and one foot out won't get it done. You have to be all in.

At times, I'll share my story and the lessons I learned in chronological order. Other times, I may jump around a bit. This is intentional—for your benefit—because there were times when I acquired insights far ahead of the curve, but there are also lessons I wish I would have learned a hell of a lot earlier. As *you* learn what it takes to Be a Pro and begin to implement this blueprint into your life, I encourage you to track your habits, track your actions, and track your growth. Analyze it. See what's working and change what isn't. Discard and upgrade.

And no, it won't happen overnight. But you'll make progress, day by day. And those days will add up to weeks, months, and years. One day, you'll wake up, and you'll have it. They will call you an "overnight success," but *you* will know better. Five or ten years from now, you'll know that what everyone's seeing is the result of years of commitment to carefully constructing the best version of yourself.

If you are still reading, I assume you're here for a reason. You *want* to get better.

You want to "max out" and fulfill your potential. You may want more success in your career. You want to realize a lifelong dream or pursue a lifelong passion. Or maybe your goal is to be a better spouse or parent. It's possible you're a young athlete who wants to reach the top levels of your sport, like I did. Maybe you've been successful in the past but have fallen off, hit a dry spell, and are trying to get back to the top (something that, as you'll soon learn, I personally struggled with). Whatever the case, **what you want is possible.** And the tools you need to get there are right here in this book.

Let the following pages serve as *your* blueprint. And as you begin to apply this blueprint, follow these principles, and implement these habits, my hope is that you'll begin to develop your own blueprint. You'll take what works best for you and tweak or discard the things that don't. I don't know what the best version of you looks like. Only you know that. Only you know what ultimate success, happiness, fulfillment, and satisfaction is for you.

It's Time to Own Your Dreams

This book will get you going, but at some point, you will have to grab the wheel and assume control for yourself. I can tell you what to do and show you the way, but it's up to you to travel that path and do the necessary work.

It will require that you cultivate a mindset of constant improvement. To develop discipline around the small, mundane actions that, when practiced daily, move the needle and get you where you want to go.

Remember: Action and execution are where the power lies. The actions necessary to take you to the next level are easy to do. But here's the kicker. They are also easy *not* to do.

This book is designed to inspire you to take action. Taking action will require that you make some sacrifices. If you want to get in better shape and improve your health, for example, you will have to exercise more and eat better. Easy to do...and easy not to do.

There is always a price to pay. You are going to pay a price for everything you do and everything you don't do. So, your choice is simple: Do the work and pay the price for success now, or don't do the work and pay the price of regret later.

Before we go any further, I want to give you permission, right here and now, to **own, pursue, and *live*** your dreams. Too many people struggle to believe that they deserve to live the life they dream of. They are afraid to own it, share it, and pursue it. The risk of failure or ridicule is too great for them.

But not for you. Not anymore.

Your dabbling ends today. Gone are the days of *trying*. Today, you begin the process of *doing*.

Today, you start Being a Pro and taking the necessary steps to make progress toward your ideal, best self.

The Playbook

To aid you in this process, I've broken this book into three sections.

Part 1 is my story. These are the lessons I learned on my journey from a ten year old with a dream, to a professional athlete, to a retired former NFL player who struggled with depression, loss of identity, purpose, and passion, and finally, to a man who found his way back on the climb to the top of another mountain. In this section, I'll introduce the three pillars of the Be a Pro blueprint: Preparation, Reliability, and Obsession, and how mastering these key pillars is crucial to creating the success, happiness, fulfillment, and achievement you are striving for.

In Part 2, I share the 33 Habits of All Pros. These are the habits, practices, and principles I believe are common among most, if not all, high performers and world-class achievers. They are a mixture of concepts that I personally used along my journey and ideas I've picked up over the course of the last decade, working with world-class athletes, CEOs, and business owners across multiple industries. I chose to include 33 very purposely. I'm a bit of a numerology nerd, and 33 is the most influential of the master numbers. It signifies expansion, advancement, and growth in everything you do.

To conclude, I share my own personal mission and purpose and encourage you to truly explore the big question: "Why am I doing this? Why am I striving to become a better version of myself?" This was a question I asked myself shortly after I retired from the NFL. The answer for me was very simple: impact. Whatever I decided to do next, I wanted to make a massive impact on the lives of others and be a part of lifting up the collective whole. Making that type of impact would require me to be my very best version of myself...someone significantly better than I'd ever been. The completion of this book, and my work in personal development, speaking, coaching, and training is due, in large part, my desire to fulfill that purpose.

CHAPTER ONE:

REALITY

January 2013

I hated the man I was looking at. I wanted to talk to him, but at the moment, my disgust for him wouldn't allow for a productive conversation, so I stayed silent.

I had known this man for years and always liked him—loved him, actually. I admired the person he had become, what he had accomplished, everything he had overcome, and the fearlessness with which he had gone after and achieved a childhood dream.

He was often considered the "underdog," and he relished that role even though he detested the word and the concept it embodied. What, just because he wasn't born with freakish athleticism and the body of a Greek god, he couldn't—or shouldn't—be a great athlete? Just because he came from a small town in Idaho not known for producing pro athletes, he couldn't be one? He took his underdog label as an insult, and he used it as motivation to prove his detractors wrong.

He was one of the hardest workers I knew. He possessed unshakeable confidence and self-assuredness, which made it almost impossible for those who knew him well to doubt him. He expected things from himself and held himself to the highest standards. I always admired him for that. He was strong, resilient, determined, and persistent.

At least, he *was*.

But over the previous few years, he had changed. He was no longer the same guy I had known. In the years since the conclusion of his football career, he had become a shell of himself.

He'd always called football his "life's work to date" and his first love. He had given almost all of his teen years and his twenties to it—nearly two-thirds of his life. He'd made countless sacrifices to overcome long odds, never doubting for a second that it was all worth it. "When you're pursuing something you love, the sacrifices aren't painful. You do it joyfully," he would always say. Back then, he would talk about how fulfilled he was by the constant quest to be better—to master his craft and be the best he could possibly be. He had direction and purpose. His life had meaning. He was living his dream.

But now, it was over. His football career had ended prematurely, and he was lost. He would have still been playing if he'd been able, but age—and a lack of interest in his services from any team—left him with no job, no purpose, no passion, no identity, and no sense of his place in the "real world." He had attempted several different business ventures, all of which had failed. Those failures had shaken his self-confidence. His mother said he was just in the process of "changing mountain tops." But the descent from his previous peak had been swift, and he'd been in the valley for too long, seeking that next mountain to climb and wondering if he even had what it took to climb another one.

Several years had passed since his last NFL paycheck. After a few bad investments and many more withdrawals than deposits on his bank account, he was now on the verge of going broke. He was in pain. Depressed, defeated, and hopeless on the inside—all the while keeping a brave face among his friends and family.

But he couldn't hide from me. I knew him better than anyone. He knew that I knew the truth. And the truth was ugly.

In the past, I had taken it upon myself to call him out on his bullshit, but lately, he rarely took the time to have those heart-to-heart conversations with me. I think he was afraid of what I might have to say. But finally, the day came when I was able to corner him. It took some time, but now that I was face to face with him, I was ready to unload on him. Regardless of how much it might hurt him, he needed to hear it.

So as I stood there, looking in the mirror, finally ready to have this conversation with myself, I knew that I needed to face the truth. I needed to admit that I was responsible for where I found myself at that moment. I had to own it. I was failing miserably, and it was my fault.

Just as I had given myself credit for much of my success in life, I had to own my failures too. I didn't like myself or my life, and I was the only one to blame. The person I had allowed myself to become was the reason I was struggling now. I wasn't having the level of success or fulfillment I had once had. And the reason was obvious.

I was no longer *doing* the things I had done to become great.

I wasn't applying any of the habits or the mindset I had once used to achieve greatness and be a high performer. I wasn't getting the results because I wasn't doing the things required. The person I had *once* been allowed me to realize a childhood dream and to live out that dream. I had a blueprint for success that was tried and true. I *knew* it worked. It was built around a deep belief in myself, an insane work ethic, consistent daily habits, goal set-

11

ting, visualization, infinite curiosity, unwavering commitment and dedication, obsession, hunger, and the desire to be my best and achieve any goal I set for myself. I made countless sacrifices and did whatever was necessary. And now, I wasn't doing any of that. I had lost my identity and lost my way because of it.

Once, I had been **a pro**. Now, I was just plain miserable.

I wasn't a high-performing pro anymore, and it was time to face the fact that who I had become was my fault. It had nothing to do with my age or the fact that my NFL career was behind me. It was because I no longer held myself to the same standards. I wasn't going after things I wanted. I was waiting for them to come to me—almost as if I now believed that success was somehow *owed* to me. Part of me believed that I had "put in my time" and done the hard work, so now things were supposed to be easy. Everything was supposed to fall into my lap. People ought to be bringing opportunities my way, opening doors for me, and serving up my next dream job or career on a silver platter.

Clearly, I had forgotten how it all began. And if I was ever going to reawaken the pro lying dormant inside me, I would need to take an objective, sobering look back.

PART I:

PREPARED, RELIABLE, AND OBSESSED

CHAPTER TWO:

GETTING STARTED

"Sharon, are you okay in there?" my dad asked through the locked bathroom door of our family home in Lewiston, Idaho.

"No, you'd better call the hospital," replied my mom, who was nine months pregnant with me at the time.

In a matter of minutes, my dad called the hospital to inform them that a baby was on the way and to send an ambulance. He then sprinted out the back door to the barn behind our house to get a nail. (Our bathroom door had one of those old locks you could pick by inserting a nail into a small hole on the front of the doorknob.) When he returned and opened the door, he was shocked to find he was too late. There stood my mom, holding me, their fifth child.

That's right. I was born on the bathroom floor.

My dad was an all-state high school football player and track athlete in Alameda, California in 1959 and 1960 and went on to play football at San Jose State University, where a knee injury during his freshman year cut his promising career short. As a kid, I can remember reading old newspaper articles he had saved in a scrapbook. I couldn't believe my dad had been such a stud athlete. He never talked about it.

My mom was extremely talented and athletic in her own right. She'd grown up in Lewiston, Idaho, and was an accomplished dancer and rodeo queen of the Lewiston Roundup. For much of my childhood, she operated a dance studio out of the basement of our home and taught tap and jazz dance to many young girls around town.

We were a traditional middle-class family of seven, living in a small town in the Pacific Northwest. I truly couldn't have asked for a better childhood. My parents provided a loving, close-knit household, and their unconditional support for all five of us kids gave us the freedom and security to go after our dreams.

My oldest brother, Mike, played football and basketball, and he excelled on the track as a 400-meter and 800-meter runner in high school. My brother Dave was a cowboy. He was an all-state team roper in high school and went to Lewis Clark State College on a rodeo scholarship. During and after college, he was consistently one of the top team ropers in the state of Idaho and the Northwest. My sisters, Lainey and Jaime, inherited my mom's love for dance. They were both accomplished tap and jazz dancers and were members of the high school dance and cheerleading teams.

Even though Mom and Dad enjoyed watching all five of their children perform in their various areas of interest, my parents' love wasn't conditional upon us accomplishing anything or being "successful." We always knew they loved and supported us no matter what. I felt this from a very young age, and because of that, I didn't fear failing.

I never shied away from going after the things I truly wanted— or expressing who I really was. And what I really wanted, from a young age, was to play football.

J. Farris, Number 56

My first baby pictures, taken when I was less than a year old, show me holding a football in my tiny hands. For the next couple of decades, a football would never be far from my grasp.

As a kid, I was a sports nut, and luckily, we were a sports family. I got a Hutch football uniform for Christmas when I was four years old, and I wore that thing everywhere. In fact, I can remember attending one of my oldest brother Mike's junior high *basketball* games fully dressed in my *football* uniform—helmet, shoulder pads, and all. Many nights, I wore my helmet at the dinner table, maneuvering a fork full of food through the face mask.

At six or seven years old, I tried on my sixteen-year-old brother's football cleats, but no matter how many pairs of socks I put on, my tiny feet just wouldn't fit into those size elevens. In despair, I had my dad help me attempt to make my own pair of cleats by gluing rocks to the bottoms of my school shoes using rubber cement. I was heartbroken when all of the rocks fell off before I even got down the stairs to the front yard.

I can vividly remember watching Monday Night Football with my dad. Having grown up in the Bay Area, he was a diehard 49ers fan, and we watched many 49ers games together when I was kid, although I tended to root for the *other* team just to be in opposition to him—one of those things that kids do sometimes, I guess. Dad would sit on the couch watching the game and throwing me passes as I repeatedly came running through the living room to catch the ball and then leap onto the couch as if diving over the goal line to score the game-winning touchdown. As for Mom, she loved watching football with us, and I owe her and my sisters everything for shuttling me to countless practices and games during the early days of my athletic career.

The Giants were my favorite team back in the day, and Lawrence Taylor was far and away my favorite player. I idolized L.T. Every year, when I got my jersey for Boys Club flag football, my mom and I would immediately take it down to the local sports store and have my name, "J. Farris," and the number 56—L.T.'s number—pressed on to the back. I did my best to play like L.T. and was convinced that one day, I would grow up to be just like him as a football player. Hell, the day after the Giants won Super Bowl XXI in 1986, I came home from school, stuffed a sleeping bag full of pillows and blankets, and made a makeshift tackling dummy so I could do my best L.T. impersonations and deliver those big hits and blind-side sacks he was famous for.

Some kids want to be Superman. I wanted to be L.T. No matter what, I was going to play professional football. I didn't really know what it would take to reach that goal and, frankly, didn't even know if it was possible. I just knew it was something I wanted to do.

Now, I won't lie to you and claim that I spent every day from that day forward focused on the goal I had set and working to achieve it. I was still a kid, through and through, and had other interests and hobbies, like most kids do. I played basketball and baseball and was equally devoted to those sports. I also loved boxing. My friends and I would often meet at one of our houses after school and box each other, then go inside and play *Mike Tyson's Punch Out!!* on Nintendo. I wanted to be Magic Johnson, Mark McGwire, and Mike Tyson as much as I wanted to be Lawrence Taylor. I had a social life with a great group of friends, and I was interested in girls and being popular like everyone else. But football was my main focus. It was my first love. Maybe the only true love of my life.

Growth

I dominated Boys and Girls Club flag football in grade school. I was fast and athletic at that age. But from age twelve to fourteen, my body didn't grow nearly as fast as my ambition, which became a problem in seventh grade, where the weight requirement to join the team was 120 pounds. Ambition notwithstanding, at barely 100 pounds, I was too small for football.

By eighth grade, I still only weighed in at 108 and stood five-foot-one. My freshman year wasn't much better. I was all of five-foot-three and 122 pounds. I still have the roster from my freshman year as evidence.

When I got to high school for my sophomore year, most people said I was too small and too slow. Nevertheless, I ended up making the varsity team as a free safety, mostly because I was a smart player and had a good understanding of the game.

Through hard work and dedication, I gained almost forty pounds over the next two years and even broke the school record for the forty-yard dash. I became an all-state wide receiver and set several school records.

My senior year, I lead my team to the state championship game. I had an outstanding game, scoring three touchdowns, but it wasn't enough, and we lost the game. I was heartbroken. Not only because we had lost but also at the realization that my high school career was over. A reporter from the local newspaper, *The Lewiston Morning Tribune*, had once written that I "had purple and gold (our school colors) in my veins," referring to my love for the program and my commitment and dedication to it. In the moments after the state championship game ended, I was hit hard with the reality I would never wear the purple and gold uniform again.

I was not highly recruited out of high school. I accepted the only scholarship offer I received from the University of Montana, aware that many people in my hometown thought I would sit on the bench for four years and soon be back in Lewiston, coaching high school football. Instead, I became an All-American wide receiver at Montana, set several records, and led my team to the national championship my senior year. In the semi-final game, I made the game-winning touchdown catch in overtime against Appalachian State that sent us to the finals. It was the highlight of my college career.

When I entered the NFL Draft in the spring of 2001, most NFL scouts gave me no chance of ever wearing an NFL uniform. But, yet again, I proved them wrong. I wasn't drafted, but I signed with the San Francisco 49ers as an undrafted free agent.

I had done it. I'd achieved the seemingly impossible goal I'd set at age ten.

A Mother's Love

Through it all, my mom was my biggest fan. One game, during my sophomore year of high school, she was standing on the sideline, just behind the team bench, watching the game. While on defense, I made an interception and was running down the sideline, trying to run it all the way back for a touchdown. The next day, when we watched the game film as a team, there was my mom, sprinting along the sideline, stride for stride with me, pumping her fists in the air and yelling, "Go, Jim!" the entire way.

Believe it or not, Mom's background as a dance teacher even came into play in my athletic career. See, I was a huge Deion Sanders fan in high school. I was a junior when Deion signed with the 49ers in 1994, and I loved Deion and wanted to do everything like him. He was famous for "high stepping" anytime he had the ball in his hands en route to the end zone. And once he scored, a touchdown dance or celebration was sure to ensue. One day, I was watching a highlight video of Deion at home that included a clip of him high stepping and doing a little dance in the end zone. Knowing what a great dancer my mom was, I asked her to show me how to do the dance. With ease, she replicated the moves and taught me, step by step, how to do it.

The next game, I caught a pass and was on my way to the end zone, and I just couldn't resist. Doing my best Deion impression, I went high stepping into the end zone, where I then did the dance Mom had taught me. There was just one problem. My coach, Nick Menegas, *despised* any type of celebration that would "show up" the opponent. He was a stickler for "acting like you've done it before." You can imagine how a man like that felt about my dance number.

I respected and admired Coach Menegas as much as any man in my life—second only to my dad. Well, after I scored that touchdown, I turned to jog back to the sideline and was met by Coach Menegas, who was not happy. He grabbed me by the face mask and said, "You're done for the night! Don't you ever pull that shit again." I sat and watched the rest of the game from the bench, sick to my stomach at the thought of disappointing him.

After the game, my mom came down onto the field and approached Coach Menegas. "I'm so sorry for what Jim did," she said.

"Oh, that's just Jimmy," said Coach. "He needed to learn a lesson. He knows I don't like that crap."

"No, but I really have to apologize," Mom said. "It's my fault... I taught him that dance."

My mom would remain my biggest fan for the remainder of my football career, right through my time in the NFL. Once, she even sent an email to Atlanta Falcons Head Coach Jim Mora asking him why I wasn't playing more. Jim told me about the email one day after practice. He thought it was great and told me how lucky I was to have a mom who cared that much and would go to bat for her son.

"It reminded me of something my own mom would do," Jim said. "You have a great mom."

I definitely do.

CHAPTER THREE:

THE MENTAL GAME

The first weekend after the draft, the 49ers, like most teams, held a mini-camp to bring the entire team together. This was the first opportunity for the new players, the rookies, and the drafted guys to interact with the veterans and the players who had already been there. It was our chance to get to know the coaching staff, the front office personnel, and the organization as a whole. It was also our first opportunity to be together as a full team.

So there I was, in April of 2001, sitting in a hotel room in Santa Clara, California, hours away from realizing my lifelong dream of making it to the NFL. I was about to take the field for the first time as a member of the San Francisco 49ers. Obviously, I was nervous and filled with anxiety. It was surreal to think back to all those autumn days as a kid, watching 49ers games with my dad and rooting for the other team. Now, I was a part of it. I was here—living out what had been a lifelong dream up to that point.

For those who may not be aware, being signed as an undrafted free agent basically means, "We like you and want you on our team, but not enough to draft you." Our first-round pick that year got an $8 million signing bonus... Mine was $5,000. That should tell you how much they thought of me! Not to belabor the point, but that's a bit like your parents getting your brother a brand-new Mercedes for his eighteenth birthday, then turning around and giving you a ten-speed bicycle for yours.

The mini-camp ran Friday, Saturday, and Sunday with two practices on Friday, two on Saturday, and one on Sunday.

While I was grateful just to be there, I went into my first NFL mini-camp with a mindset that I was going to show them that I was ready to be an NFL player—that I had put in the work, and now that I'd finally gotten this opportunity, I was going to prove it'd been a mistake not to draft me.

Still, I was a bit uneasy. Yes, I had signed a contract, but that didn't necessarily mean I would make the final roster. I *knew* that in order to make the team, I was going to have to be a good punt returner. I was confident in my abilities as a wide receiver, but I wasn't going to be a starter at receiver. They already had several excellent wide receivers, including an All-Pro wide receiver by the name of Terrell Owens—maybe you've heard of him. In fact, I can vividly remember sitting at my locker, getting ready for my first practice, when Terrell Owens walked in.

I had imagined the moment I would meet T.O. ever since signing my rookie contract with the 49ers the week before. Here was that moment, and I'll admit, I couldn't help but stare. He was even bigger, taller, more ripped, and more superhero-like than I'd expected him to be. I was caught in the awkward moment many rookies experience of attempting to reconcile being a fan with now being a *teammate* of a superstar.

I had been an All-American wide receiver in college and was coming off an amazing senior season. At the college level, I'd been great. But that day, I remember thinking, *Man, if this is what NFL receivers look like, I might as well turn in my gear right now.*

While Terrell Owens and I played the same position, our places on the team were very different. He was one of the best wide receivers in the league—guaranteed to make the roster and be a starter. I was guaranteed that day. One practice, and nothing more. I knew that if I was going to make the team, I was going to have to excel at special teams—particularly as a punt returner.

Anytime you're watching football and you see the ball being kicked off, or a field goal attempt, or a punt, you're watching special teams in action. Special teams is also referred to as the kicking game, and it's an integral yet often overlooked component of football. Coaches know that special teams is just as important as offense or defense, especially considering that it accounts for about one third of the game. The problem for me was that I hadn't returned punts in a live game since high school. So although I had caught plenty of punts in practice during my college career, it had been almost five years since I had done it in a pressure situation.

So here I was, on my first day, auditioning to be a punt returner for the 49ers...and I felt totally unprepared.

After our second of two practices on Day One, the coaches had all of us who were trying out to be punt returners stay to catch some punts. It was their first chance to get a look at us in action. Some of the other rookies had done this in college and had done it really well, so I already knew I was behind the eight ball.

As I crossed the field with the rest of this group of rookies—all of whom were trying out for the same position I was trying out for—I remember thinking, *Okay, this is it. If this doesn't go well, this could be it for me.* I prayed that I could somehow look good in this drill and do a good job. If not, my NFL career could begin and end on the same day.

Now, standing all by yourself, trying to catch a ball that a punter has just kicked what feels like two miles into the air is difficult enough. Add in the fact that some of the baddest, meanest, toughest dudes in all of professional sports are, at the same time, running down the field, trying to knock your head clean off your body, and you've got yourself a scary proposition. A punt return is the Stephen King horror movie of football.

I watched a couple of the other guys catch some punts ahead of me and tried to get a feel for their technique to see if I could pick anything up. I had the positive self-talk going, trying to remind myself that I was the man, that I was a stud—that I was *good enough* to do this!

Well, finally, it was my turn, so I confidently stepped up, acting like I'd done this a million times. You know, "Fake it till you make it." I watched the ball come off the punter's foot, tracked it as it flew high into the air, ran to the spot where I thought it would come down, settled under it, slowly brought my arms up to gently cradle it in, nice and relaxed, kept my eyes focused on it, and—*BOOM!* The ball hit me right in the face and went flying about twenty yards in front of me.

Some of the guys were laughing. Some of the coaches were cringing. Of course, I did what any self-respecting stud would do and tried to play it off like I'd meant to do it. But you can imagine my reaction.

I was humiliated. Here I was, supposed to be a professional football player, and I'd just gotten hit in the face with a football. I got a couple more opportunities, and I managed to get it together a little bit and at least catch the ball. But the reality was, I did not look good in that drill. It was clear that I was not a good punt returner.

After practice, we were all headed into the locker room. I was worried that I might've just blown my whole opportunity to show the coaches that I could play.

As I was walking in, Coach George Stewart walked up next to me, put his arm around me, and said, "How you feeling? What are you thinking?"

I said, "Man, I just blew it."

"You didn't return punts in college, did you?" he said, confirming that my inexperience had been transparent.

"No, I didn't," I admitted.

"Did you practice at all leading up to this mini-camp, knowing that you were going to have to do this and be good at it in order to make this team?"

The truth, which I didn't tell him at the time, was that I honestly thought I would be able to get by with my current skill level... I was betting that I was good enough to make it through the first mini-camp. What I did tell him was that I couldn't find a punter to kick to me, and even if I had, springtime in Montana was frigid with temperatures in the teens with snow and ice still covering much of the ground. The conditions of the field in our outdoor stadium were not conducive to getting any real, quality practice time in. Stew listened patiently but was clearly not impressed with my excuses.

"Well, here is what I'll tell you," said Coach Stew. "We obviously thought you were a good player in college. We signed you to a contract and gave you an opportunity. You were good enough to get here. But what you need to understand is that **what got you here won't keep you here.** I know it's only your first day, but you are not an amateur anymore; you're in the pros."

That's the polite version of what Coach Stew said, anyway. He went on to say, "This is pro football. Motherfuckers get paid to do this. If you want to stay here, you have got to take everything to another level. No excuses, no bullshit. You have got to learn how to be a pro."

Be a pro. It was the first time I had ever heard that phrase. But as soon as he said it, I knew exactly what he meant—I needed to get better...to *be* better.

I had come in with this mentality that I was good enough. Hell, that's what I'd been thinking when I'd stepped up to catch that punt. That I was "good enough" to do this. I was going to show them that I was ready. That I was a player. And on my first day, I basically showed them the opposite.

Coach Stew's message got through loud and clear. If I wanted to stay here, have a career in the NFL, and be a 49er, I would have to adopt a mindset of consistent, daily improvement, regardless of how "good" I thought I already was.

I was not an amateur anymore. I had to learn how to be a pro.

Shifting The Mindset

Making it to the NFL was a goal I always knew I would achieve. I had been working hard for it. But I had a little chip on my shoulder because I hadn't been drafted. I remember feeling a little bit slighted. It was the same chip on my shoulder that I had going into college.

As I mentioned earlier, my only recruitment offer had come from the University of Montana. While Montana was still deciding whether or not to offer me a football scholarship, Head Coach Mick Dennehy came to meet with me and my high school coach in my coach's office.

"I think you're a great player," said Mick. "You're tough. You catch the ball really well. But at this point, I don't feel like you're fast enough or have the type of explosion needed in order to be a big-time player at our level in our league. So as of right now, we've got a couple other kids we're going to offer scholarships to who are a little bit faster, more explosive, and a bit more athletic than you are. So if one of them turns our offer down or chooses to go to another school, we'll come back and offer it to you."

Basically, he was saying, "You're good, just not quite good enough."

The University of Montana did end up coming back and offering me a scholarship later, which I accepted. But I never got over initially feeling like he didn't think I was good enough, or fast enough, to be an impact player. I spent my entire college career trying to prove Mick Dennehy wrong.

Going into that 49ers camp, I had that same mentality: "I am going to prove to these guys wrong (for not drafting me) and show them that I am good enough. That mindset had served me well in college. It was the catalyst to much of my success in football to that point. But the revelation, now that I was a pro, was that my mindset needed to shift from "I'm here to prove to you guys I'm good enough" to "I'm here to humble myself a bit and get better."

I quickly learned that I had a lot of work to do. And there were a lot of people around me who could help me get better.

If I'm smart, I realized, *I will totally open my mind up to everything that they're teaching me, take advantage of all the resources I have, get better, and take my game to another level.*

I'd signed with the 49ers. I was in practice. I was wearing the helmet. But I hadn't really accomplished anything. Not yet, anyway.

The realization for me was that my big vision—getting to the NFL—wasn't big *enough*. Because it wasn't just about getting there. The real vision was to live out the goal.

This is a subtle yet important mindset shift adopted by high performers. They work hard to fulfill their vision, but once they meet their goals, that's when the real work begins to try to be better. And that, to me, is a fundamental difference between amateurs and pros: amateurs celebrate achieving the goal, but pros understand that the initial achievement is just the beginning.

In little over a decade since retiring form the NFL, my work with world-class performers has led me to uncover a number of these subtle differences in mindset between these pros and the amateurs. Look at the examples in the charts below and take a moment to evaluate yourself. In which areas do you have a pro mindset? In which areas do you need to upgrade your mindset?

Amateur Mindset:

- "I'm already good enough."
- Sees coaching and feedback as criticism and is prone to take it personally
- Values isolated performances
- Gives up or loses interest when faced with adversity or failure
- Thinks knowledge is power
- Blames others
- Makes suggestions but defers to others
- Focuses on being right
- Stops when the goal is achieved

Pro Mindset:

- "There is always more to learn and room to grow and get better."
- Knows they have weaknesses and welcomes coaching and feedback
- Values consistency
- Sees adversity and failure as part of the process
- Knows action is where the power lies
- Takes responsibility ("I am the problem; I am the solution.")
- Makes decisions

- Focuses on getting the right/best outcome
- Knows the initial achievement is just the beginning

I could cite hundreds more examples, but hopefully the list above gives you a general understanding of some of the key differences between the pro and amateur mindsets. There is no doubt I was an amateur when I took the field for my first practice with the 49ers, but with the help of Coach Stew, I began to make the shift. And in doing so, I was able to get better...quickly!

And by the way, I did eventually learn how to catch a punt. Before practice the next morning, I met Coach Stew on the field to begin to learn the finer details of the trade. Before we began, we talked about what had gone wrong the previous day. I'll never forget his instructions: "You looked it in, didn't you?" he said, referring to my failed attempt.

"Yes, I watched it all the way."

"What were you looking at?"

"The *ball!*"

It was clear to Coach Stew at that point that I didn't know how to "read" a punt.

"Well, that's part of the problem," said Coach Stew. "You only need to focus on that front point of the ball. If it stays up, the ball will fall straight down and to your right a little. If it turns over and points down at you, it is going to carry a bit further and curve back to the left a little...and that is why it hit you in the face. You need to catch at least a thousand punts before training camp starts. You're a pro now. Practice your craft."

Man, this is great advice, I thought. *This is what NFL-level coaching looks like. This is awesome!*

And then he gave me some of the most practical advice I've ever gotten as a professional: "Just relax." He knew that while I lacked some of the necessary skills to be great a punt returner, the biggest obstacle was mental—a lack of confidence. I would physically tense up waiting for the ball to be kicked, worried I wouldn't be able to make the catch. To loosen me up a bit, Stew said whenever you run out there to catch a punt, and you're waiting for the ball to be kicked, say this little phrase to yourself. (And I kid you not, this is no joke... An NFL coach taught me this...)

"Porkchop, porkchop, greasy, greasy. Catching these punts is easy, easy."

Like Father, Like Son

Despite my laser focus on getting better and reaching the next level, there were still times when I looked around and reminded myself how grateful I was to be where I was.

One day, during my rookie year with the 49ers, while at training camp in Stockton, California—at the University of the Pacific, about eighty miles from the Bay Area—I was walking off the field into the locker room when a man approached the fence surrounding the field and shouted my name. It was common for fans to flock to the practice fields to watch the team practice on those hot summer days, but as a rookie, I was surprised to hear someone shouting *my* name. The guy got my attention, and I walked over to the fence to talk with him.

"Is your dad Bobby Farris?" the man asked.

"Maybe," I replied with an awkward laugh.

My dad's name is Robert, and he goes by Bob. I had never heard him called Bobby before.

"Did he go to Alameda High?" the man asked.

"Yes, he did!" I said.

"Oh man, I played high school football with your dad," the man said excitedly and told me his name. "Please tell your dad I said hello. He'll remember me!"

"I'll do it," I said.

Before he walked away, the man added, seemingly as an afterthought, "Let me tell you something. I've been watching you out here for a few days now, and you're a great player, but you ain't got shit on your old man. *He* was a great player!" My dad *was* great, and I was happy to assume the position as the second-best football player in the family.

My heart was full of pride that day. Here I was, pursuing my dream with the same pro football team my dad grew up watching and cheering for, in his old stomping grounds in Northern California.

After our first preseason game against the Chargers a week later, I spoke with my dad on the phone. He and my mom had watched the game on TV from home. He told me that when he saw me out on the field with that 49ers helmet on, he had to pinch himself to make sure it was real. I could hear the pride in his voice and was overcome with emotion.

I hung up the phone and went back to my dorm room and cried.

CHAPTER FOUR:

BE PREPARED

Get Clarity
Make a Plan
Attend to Detail
Cultivate Self-Discipline

Prepare: to make ready beforehand for some purpose, use, or activity.

The story of my first day with the 49ers in the previous chapter illustrates several key points. One is the importance of cultivating a mindset of growth and constant improvement—what I refer to as the Pro Mindset. You've already taken the first steps to improving your own mindset by evaluating where your mindset lines up with the pros and where your mindset lines up with the amateurs. The second point of the story is the value in being prepared. Former Secretary of State, James Baker, was once quoted as saying, "Proper preparation prevents poor performance." I couldn't agree with him more. I was NOT prepared to the best of my ability on that first day, and it nearly cost me my career.

In this chapter, we will delve into what proper preparation looks like in a practical sense, how you can develop this skill, and how to apply it to multiple areas of your life and business. But first, a romantic tragedy.

When I was in the sixth grade, I had a huge crush on a girl in my class. Her name was Jennifer.

Jennifer was amazing. Beautiful, smart, great style, the whole package (or at least as much of the whole package as an eleven year old could be). I was desperate to get her to be my girlfriend. But, to my dismay, she just wasn't that interested. She had her eyes on another boy in our class. Nick Williams.

Now, Nick and I were friends, but I was miffed by the fact that he had seemingly won Jennifer's heart, and I was the odd man out. By this time in my life, my competitive nature was already fully developed, so I took this as a challenge to "beat him out" for her love. I was going to show her that I was the best "man" for her. So I did the usual things sixth graders do. Left notes in her desk. Drew her cute pictures. Told her she looked beautiful every day. But none of it worked.

Around springtime every year at my grade school, they held a mini Olympics of sorts. It was called Field Day and consisted of track and field events out on the playground for students of each grade level to participate in. At this time in my life, the only thing I was in love with more than Jennifer was sports, and I considered myself to be a good athlete, so there was no doubt I was always one of the first kids to sign up for as many events as were allowed. I already wanted to win and prove I was the best...at everything.

That motivation to be the best only grew when I saw that Nick and I were signed up for several of the same events. *Here's my chance*, I thought. *My chance to show Jennifer, once and for all, that I am, in fact, the best man for her.*

I devised a plan to ensure that I would win every event in which Nick and I would compete. I wasn't about to leave this up to chance. I was going to be prepared. I would outwork him leading up to Field Day, and he wouldn't stand a chance.

Every day after school for a month, I ran one mile around the block in the Lewiston Orchards. I did pushups and sit-ups in the backyard to guarantee I would be in the best shape possible. I visualized myself winning each race and getting that coveted blue ribbon for first place.

When the day of the event finally came, I was so excited. I knew I was prepared and all I had to do was perform. And I did. I won all my events, and I beat Nick in our head-to-head events. I remember feeling so satisfied and proud of myself. The work I had put in to be prepared paid off.

Now, you're probably wondering if I also won the girl that day. The answer is...no, I didn't. My athletic triumphs didn't change her mind one bit. But all was not lost. I learned one of the most valuable lessons of my young life. Those events planted the seed in my mind for the importance and value of proper preparation. I had a goal, I put a plan in place to achieve it, and I did it. Most of it, anyway.

You Never Know What You Might Get Into

When I was in college, I heard a story about Deion Sanders carrying $5,000 in cash on him at all times. He had started doing this while he was still playing college football at Florida State after he had signed an MLB contract. His reason for this, as he said, was because "you never know what you might get into." I just loved that mentality... I thought it was great. So, naturally, once I started making a little money, I wanted to adopt a similar "policy."

When I signed my first NFL contract with the 49ers and got my signing bonus of a whopping $5,000, I thought I was rich! After taxes, it was around $4,000—not enough for Deion Sanders pocket money. Nevertheless, I decided I was going to be as much like Deion as I could be and carry $1,000 on me at all times.

Initially, my friends made fun of me ruthlessly over this. They were just *hoping* I would get mugged and beaten up in an alley so I would get the message and realize what a terrible idea it was to carry that much cash. In their minds, there was *no* situation that would ever require anyone to have $1,000 in cash on hand. Small minds, I tell ya!

Later that summer, I was out at a bar with a bunch of friends when one of my buddies came running in and told me that one of my *best* friends, who was supposed to be meeting us, was in a fight out in the parking lot. Naturally, I ran outside too and found him in the middle of the first fight of his life. The fight wasn't pretty. Neither guy really connected, and luckily, no one was injured. Within a few minutes, the police came, arrested them both, and hauled them down to the station.

About twenty minutes later, my friend called to inform me that his first fistfight earned him a comfy seat in jail, and he needed to be bailed out. He told me he had no money on him and certainly couldn't call his parents. He told me if me and the other guys couldn't come up with the money, he was going to spend the night in jail. (You can see where I'm going with this...)

"About how much is it going to take to bail you out?" I asked.

When he told me it was $800, I started smiling. Grinning ear to ear, I told him I'd talk to the rest of the guys and call him back.

When I hung up, everyone started asking me what the deal was, so I proceeded to tell them about the $800 bail. Everyone started searching their pockets, coming up with fives, tens, and twenties. All told, I think they came up with $70 or $80.

Finally, one of my friends looked up at me and said, "Hey, wait a minute! Don't you always carry $1,000 on you?"

I was like, "Yeah, baby!"

Vindication at last!

We went down to the station, bailed him out, and went back to the bar and had a great night. To this day, when I get together with my friends back home, they still ask me if I have $1,000 on me, and we all laugh out loud together! As Deion says, "You never know what you might get into!" Always be prepared.

As I grew older and took on bigger challenges in life and athletics, I continued to apply the same mindset I had exercised as a sixth grader—and, later, as a rookie with cash in his pocket. Be prepared. But what I also came to realize over the years was that there was a specific *way* to prepare. There was a method to preparation. A certain process that needed to be followed in order to ensure your preparation would be fruitful. And that process is as follows:

1. Get a clear vision of what you want
2. Put a plan in place for how you're going to get it
3. Work the plan and outwork the competition

And that's all there is to it.

Again, this process is simple but not easy. And if you can master it, the results can be incredible.

The first step is to be absolutely clear about what you want. What is your desired outcome or destination?

Let's dive in.

Vision

I have always had big dreams—a vision for my life of things I wanted to accomplish and the person I wanted to become.

These days, if you attend one of my seminars, you will hear me speak at length about the importance of having a vision for your life that's better than your current situation or circumstances. I believe everyone has this in some fashion. Your vision may not be as detailed or defined as others', but somewhere, deep down, you know you want better for yourself and your family, and you have a vision of what it would like if you achieved that.

People often think of a "vision" as some grand, ethereal concept. Unfortunately, that means that visions are often treated as little more than childlike, wish-upon-a-star fantasies.

In reality, **a vision is simply a goal.** Granted, it's an enormous, intricate, multilayered goal, but it's a goal, nonetheless.

I believe that having a vision, or a set of goals, is absolutely crucial if you want to realize any degree of happiness, success, and fulfillment. In my extensive and multifaceted experiences working alongside world-class athletes and high performers across many industries, I've rarely met a pro who doesn't agree.

But having a vision or a set of goals isn't enough. You must also have a strategy or plan for how you are going to make it come to fruition. This is the key element that many people miss. Any goal or dream, large or small, will require a plan of some sort in order to achieve it. There is a process that must be followed.

This process begins with getting clarity.

The Three Ps of Clarity

Knowing *exactly* what you are preparing for is a key first step to being the most prepared you can be. Thus, you must have clarity of purpose (what), person (who), and plan (how). I call these the Three Ps of Clarity:

1. **Clarity of Purpose:** What do you want, why are you doing it, and where are you trying to go?
2. **Clarity of Person:** Who do you need to be or become in order to achieve the goal or reach the destination?
3. **Clarity of Plan:** How, *specifically*, are you going to get the goal or reach the destination?

Clarity of Purpose

In my experience with high performers, one thing has become evident: they are all extremely clear about what they want. They know what they want, and they know why they want it. In *The 7 Habits of Highly Effective People*, Stephen Covey refers to this as beginning with the end in mind. **Having clarity about your destination allows you to plot the course to getting there.**

I am old enough to remember what life was like before smartphones. I didn't get my first cell phone until I was twenty-one, and back then, cell phones weren't very "smart," especially compared to the supercomputers we carry in our pockets today.

Out of all the amazing technology and apps on my phone right now, one of my favorites is the Maps application. It's brilliant. You simply type in your destination, and it calculates the route and gives you precise directions on how to get there. But imagine, for a moment, how useless and ineffective that app would be if it didn't know where you were trying to go. How could it give you directions if you hadn't input a clear, well-defined destination?

As an athlete, it was always incredibly important that I trained to continually improve and get better, but it was even more important that I was focusing on improving the right things—the skills that were necessary to be great at my specific job. I needed my workout plan to address the areas relevant to my position.

As a wide receiver, it was important to be quick, fast, explosive, agile, lean, and well-conditioned. That was my clear objective. The size of my muscles, for example, was beneficial but not nearly as crucial as the items listed above. As a wide receiver, being able to bench five hundred pounds was not as important to me as running a 4.4 forty-yard dash.

My goal, my clear objective, every offseason was to prepare myself to be a great wide receiver. If I had spent an entire offseason training my ass off with the offensive linemen, lifting heavy weights, bulking up, and getting strong as on ox, would I have been prepared? Sure. But I would have been prepared for the wrong thing.

You can work yourself to death every day and *still* get nowhere if you're working toward the wrong goal. It is important to know exactly what you want or where you're trying to go.

That is the purpose of your preparation. Without extreme clarity about that, it is nearly impossible to get the desired outcome.

Clarity of Person

Anytime we set a goal, we tend to think about what we will have to *do* in order to achieve the goal. Rarely do we ask the more important question: **Who do I need to *be*?**

What we do on a daily basis, whether consciously or unconsciously, shapes who we are. Poor diet and exercise habits tend to make us overweight and unhealthy. Poor study habits make us subpar students in the classroom. Our habits shape who we are and shape our reality. For the most part, I think the average person innately understands this concept. The problem is, they tend to put in much of the work on the wrong side of the equation.

So, along with "What do I need to do?", the question that high performers frequently ask themselves is, "Who do I need to be?" This question leads them to imagine a future, better version of themselves. A version that is capable of achieving the goal they've set. By merely imagining yourself as the person you want to become, you're more likely to begin to exhibit those characteristics and actively engage in becoming that future version of yourself. The habits, therefore, come more naturally.

Do you want to be more honest, kinder, or more loving toward your family and friends? Then start right now by *being* those things. You don't have to wait until "some time" in the distant future. You can be intentional about who you want to become and begin to *be* that person right now—today. Imagining who you need to be and then consistently exhibiting the traits of that future (better) version of yourself will lead you to *become* that person.

When I was a fifteen-year-old sophomore in high school, I played on the varsity football team, which was rare at Lewiston High School at that time. But, while I was skilled enough to have made the team, I was also 150 pounds, frail, slow, and not a superb athlete. I knew that if I was going to realize the kind of success I had envisioned for myself as a player, I would need to get much better physically.

After that season ended, I had a talk with my coach, Nick Menegas. (You'll remember Coach Menegas from earlier in this book. He was the guy who benched me for dancing in the endzone.) At that time in my life, Coach Menegas was a football god to me. In my mind, no one understood the game better than he did.

I trusted his opinion and advice more than anyone when it came to football. In our conversation, I expressed to him that I wanted to be a two-way starter next season, make the all-state team, and eventually get a college scholarship. "What do I need to do to make that happen?" I asked. He told me I needed to get bigger, faster, stronger, smarter, and tougher. But what he said next was what stuck with me and shaped my life as an athlete moving forward.

"In order to do that," he said, "you will have to *be* disciplined, dedicated, and extremely committed in the weight room, on the track, and with your diet."

Coach Menegas told me what I would need to do, but, more importantly, he told me who I would need to *be*. The *what* (lifting weights, running sprints, eating thousands of calories, studying film) didn't matter if I wasn't the type of person who was willing to do it. In order to do those things, I would need to *be* someone different than the person I'd been up to that point.

The next day, I got up early and got in a lifting session before school started. I packed two sandwiches and some snacks in my backpack—one to eat between breakfast and lunch and one to eat between lunch and dinner. I even started setting an alarm for 1:00 a.m. to get up and eat another sandwich I'd made before going to bed, all to ensure that I was consuming enough calories to gain weight and get stronger.

I joined the track team that spring to work on increasing my speed. I also began watching game film to study our plays and the plays of our opponents. I *became* a disciplined, dedicated, committed person because that's what was necessary to achieve the goal. Coach Menegas gave me Clarity of Person—an understanding of who I would need to be—and I went about becoming that person.

If you don't have extreme Clarity of Person at the moment, don't worry. It's not something innate; rather, it's something you must develop. It won't reveal itself on its own. You have to seek it. Asking questions, trying new things, seeking opportunities, and getting outside of your comfort zone will help bring about the clarity you need.

I also recommend studying people who are already doing what you want to do. See who they are and study what they do that makes them great at it. This will help you determine who you need to become and will provide you with the clarity to discover that future version of yourself.

Clarity of Plan

Think back to the last time you bought a piece of furniture from a big-box store. You know the sort of furniture I'm talking about—the kind that comes in a box without a single inch to spare, with a notice that says "some assembly required" and a set of instructions printed in English and Swedish. But even though this supposedly large piece of furniture is contained within a box that appears *way* too small, you know there's no reason to panic. The instructions they provide will show you exactly how to create what you need. In short, you've got a plan.

Now, imagine if the store sent you home with the wrong set of assembly instructions. The instructions could be perfectly accurate, but if they're the wrong set of instructions—directions for assembling a piece of furniture other than the one you bought—then you won't get you the outcome you desire.

As an aside, I'm not even sure that the assembly instructions provided by these types of stores are as clear as they could be... These instructions are produced with the intent that anyone, in any country, speaking any language, would be able to understand them. As a result, the instructions are picture-based, which, depending on how you learn best, might not be the best option for you. In fact, it could be downright confusing.

In any case, if you follow the wrong instructions—or a set of instructions communicated in a way that is not ideal for you—you can be certain that your "furniture" will *not* look the way it did in the showroom. To build something, you've got to have a plan in place, and **it's got to be the right plan.**

One of the hallmarks of high performers is that they put a plan in place to guide them toward their goal or vision. I feel that this is the key factor of success that a lot of people fail to address.

All you have to do is peruse social media around the first of January to see that the average person has no problem setting a goal. Fewer people develop a clear vision of what they want their outcome to be. And even fewer take the time to define who they need to be to make it happen. But what really separates pros from amateurs is the initiative to put an actual plan in place. This is a key component of realizing your goal or vision.

No matter how much passion and drive you possess, you can't go to a bank and ask for $100,000 to start a business without a business plan. They won't even give you a meeting if you don't have a business plan. Too many people are treating their life in the same way. They aren't taking the time to consciously write out a detailed plan, a step-by-step strategy on how they are going to get from where they are to where they want to go.

The Right Plan

So, you've established your Clarity of Plan, and you're excited to get started. But hold up! Before you start executing, the next step is to examine your plan down to the most extreme, tiniest detail.

45

Here again I have to stress the importance of committing to the *right* plan, specifically for your stated outcome. This takes time, but trust me. It's worth it.

Let's say your goal is to get in shape, so you go to the gym and hire a personal trainer. Your trainer is going to sit down with you for a consultation *before* any of the real work begins. Before you start working out, he or she will ask you, "What is your goal? What do you want to do?" Why? Because a sixteen-year-old kid who needs to gain ten to fifteen pounds of muscle is going to require a very different plan than a thirty-five-year-old mother of two who wants to lose that extra twenty pounds she's been carrying since giving birth to her first child. (And if your trainer *does* recommend the same plan for those two people, head for the door!)

It is not enough to say you want to work out and get in shape because working out and getting in shape can look many different ways and mean many different things to different people. The specific outcome you want is going to determine your exact plan. And if you want to have massive success and really get the outcome you desire, the plan that you are following needs to be highly specialized for you and highly specific to your intended outcome.

In my business coaching practice I work with executives and business owners every day who tell me how hard they're working to improve their businesses, yet they aren't getting the results they need or expected. They have put a plan in place to boost sales and increase profits. They have worked the plan from every angle and spent long hours at the office, ensuring that no detail is overlooked. But a deeper dive into what they are actually doing often reveals that they are, in fact, working hard at the wrong things. This could be because they haven't taken the necessary time to gain true Clarity of Purpose. Or it could simply mean that the plan they have in place isn't the ideal solution for getting them where they are ultimately trying to go.

The takeaway: It's not enough to have a plan or strategy in place. It has to be the *right* plan for your specific, stated outcome.

When I was a football player, one of my favorite days of the week during the football season was Wednesday—the day we got our "game book." This hardcover three-ring binder contained the game plan—a collection of all of the plays we would run in the game on Sunday.

This was our plan of attack, so to speak, and it was put together by coaches and staff after hundreds of hours of film study and scouting of our upcoming opponent. It was full of scouting reports on the opposing team's players and their tendencies and laid out exactly how we planned to move the football, score points, and win the game. From a tactical standpoint, everything we needed to *prepare* to win the game was included in that game book.

Naturally, I wanted to be as prepared as possible to ensure the greatest probability of success for myself and for the team as a whole, so I would spend hours poring over the details of the game plan. As a team, we would spend three days of practice that week repping and rehearsing the plays contained in the game plan so we could be sharp and ready to execute on Sunday.

And finally, on game day, if we carried out the plan successfully, we would be victorious.

I can't stress this enough: Knowing the importance of the game plan, and the level to which coaches and players depend on that plan, it's impossible not to see the importance of it being the *right* plan.

Imagine a scenario where my teammates and I were going into a game against the Seahawks, but we had mistakenly been given a game book that contained our plan for the Cowboys the following week. Would we be prepared as best we could to win? No. We would have spent hours practicing and preparing—but for the wrong opponent. Regardless of how hard we had worked that week in practice, how diligently we studied, and how well we executed, our likelihood of success would have been significantly reduced.

One more example... Let's say your goal is to save a million dollars for retirement. You can put a plan in place to save five hundred bucks a month. You're now saving money. Good job! But is that going to get you to a million dollars?

Hard to say. It *could* work for a twenty-five year old with the right knowledge and some wise investing. When you factor in compounding interest and the historical returns in the market, yes, the twenty-five year old who saves and wisely invests $500 a month could eventually get a million dollars.

But let's assume you are older than twenty-five. Let's say you're thirty years old. That plan no longer works for you. You are five years behind. *Your* plan might need to be $750 a month to get to a million by the time you're age sixty-five.

You can't just follow somebody else's strategy. One person's perfect plan might not be specific to you, your situation, your age, or your goals. The point is to create something that works for you.

With that being said, I want to make it clear that it's okay if you don't currently know what the *right* plan is for you. If that's the case, what's most important is that you put a plan in place and take action.

I know this might sound slightly contradictory, but sometimes, just getting started is half the battle. **Don't get bogged down in a period of inactivity while you wait until you have the perfect plan in place.** The right plan is crucial, but paralysis by analysis is something to be avoided. Having *a* plan and getting started, at the very least, is better than no plan at all.

Often times, the *right* plan will develop over time, through trial and error, so it's important that you stay flexible and open to change. Too many people stay married to their original plan and refuse to make slight corrections or adjustments when it's clear that is what's needed.

CHAPTER FIVE:

SELF-DISCIPLINE

In the previous chapter, we talked about the importance of effective preparation. Most people will find it easy to follow the guidance I've provided pertaining to clarity and developing the right plan—that is, when they're feeling motivated.

Anything will come easy when you *feel* like doing it. But what happens when your initial motivation starts to taper off? What happens when you no longer *feel* like sticking to your plan? Well, self-discipline is the glue that holds together the entire concept of being prepared.

Without self-discipline, very few of the things you want to accomplish in life are possible. You can be clear on exactly what you want, have the ideal plan in place, and still accomplish nothing because you aren't disciplined enough to consistently take the appropriate, necessary action, day in and day out.

So, what exactly is self-discipline? When you distill this characteristic down to its essentials, self-discipline is the ability to **consistently do what needs to be done, regardless of how you feel.**

When motivations fails, discipline prevails.

This is why self-discipline trumps motivation. Most people want to be motivated. They want to *feel* like doing the task at hand. But how you feel about doing something that needs to be done is not important. Getting it done is.

If you have to wait until you feel like doing something—in other words, until you're motivated—the chances are slim that you will ever be able to make progress in becoming your best self. This is a trait that is present in high performers that truly separates them from their lower-performing peers. Just like everyone else, high performers don't always feel motivated. The difference is, they simply don't let their feelings get in the way of completing the task at hand.

My friends, family, and coaching clients have all heard me say at one time or another: **"Don't let your feelings get in the way."** In other words, don't let your lack of motivation, energy, or "want-to-do" prevent you from doing the things you need to do.

To Do and Not To Do

Discipline comes in several forms. There is the discipline to do what needs to be done, and there's the discipline not to do, or to stop doing, the things that aren't moving you closer to what you want. My career as an athlete taught me that both forms are of equal importance.

The summer before my sophomore year of high school, I started to spend a good deal of time with a group of friends who were heading into their senior year. They were athletes and going to be starters on the varsity team that upcoming season. I saw them as the guys I was trying to be like. At that moment, they were where I wanted to be.

Every morning that summer, they would pick me up and take me to the weight room to work out with the varsity football team. We would lift weights, run, and then get on the field for some football-specific work. While most of them had spots secured on the team, I was in the process of trying to earn my spot. I loved working out with them and seeing what it took to be a varsity athlete. Some of these guys were the best football players I knew personally, and I was watching their every move so as to look and act the part as much as possible. I was nowhere near the biggest, fastest, or strongest kid around. I was a decent athlete, but I had miles to go in nearly every measurable athletic category if I was going to have any chance of playing varsity football that season, let alone become a good enough player to get a college scholarship in a few short years.

These intense morning workouts were critical to my physical improvement, but I was also building my mental strength. I was building the self-discipline necessary to *do* all the things I would need to do to be the best I could possibly be...for that season and all the seasons to come.

At the same time, I was also establishing my social life. I was leaving junior high and about to enter into high school, where I was hopeful of being a popular, well-liked kid. I started spending most weekends with my new friends, going to the best parties attended by all the upperclassmen I hoped would become my friends. But popularity and a thriving social life also meant increased demands placed on my self-discipline.

At one point that summer, I was at a party and was offered a beer for the first time. Of course, not wanting to face the ridicule of turning it down, I quickly grabbed it and opened it.

At that moment, multiple thoughts went through my mind. *How will I look if I drink this? How will I look if I don't? Do I have to drink this to look "cool"?* But the question I asked myself that ultimately made the decision for me was, *Will drinking this have an impact on me as an athlete?* And while I didn't know at that time what the effects of alcohol on athletic performance were, I knew enough to know that it would not *help* me. I turned away from the group, set the beer down, and made the decision that I wasn't going to drink. Ever. I am proud to say that I had my first alcoholic drink of any kind on my thirty-first birthday, a full year after I retired from the NFL. (Oh, and not drinking didn't make me any less cool with my friends. They respected me and applauded me for my choice.)

Choosing not to drink was just one of many things I *didn't* do during my pursuit of athletic excellence. I avoided drugs, fast food—even sex for years. I never once missed a workout or short-changed a set or a rep within a workout. I constantly monitored myself to make sure my lifestyle was congruent with my goals. I built my discipline around things I consistently did and didn't do. And the things I *didn't* do were every bit as important as the things I did.

Plant, Cultivate, Harvest

Now that we've defined self-discipline and examined why it's such an important character trait in high performers, let me break the bad news to you...

Self-discipline is boring.

It's true. Doing the small, seemingly insignificant things on a daily basis is *not* exciting. And when viewed only from a short-term perspective, you may ask yourself if what you are doing really matters. Will eating this one cheeseburger or missing this one workout *really* hurt me? Probably not. But when viewed from a long-term perspective, it absolutely matters. After a few months of continually eating that cheeseburger and missing that workout, you *will* wake up overweight and out of shape. On the flip side, after a few months of choosing healthy meals and working out four times a week, you will begin to see the body you want.

One of the major problems that people have pertaining to self-discipline is that it rarely results in instant gratification. In today's push-button, on-demand society, people want things now. Waiting a week for the next episode of your favorite show is unbearable—"I want to know how it ends *now*." We have forgotten the element of time that is involved.

We have seemingly forgotten the concept of **planting, cultivating, and harvesting**. A patient farmer knows a seed planted in the spring must be cultivated for months before it is ready for harvest. It would be absurd for him to plant a seed today and expect to harvest in a few days. But that is what we have come to as a society. We get a gym membership, begin working out, and are discouraged and disappointed that we aren't buff and ripped within a week. We don't see the instant results, so we quit and go in search of the latest pill or shake that will surely get us those quick results. Why spend years working, saving, and investing to be a millionaire when I can buy a lottery ticket and potentially have it now?

Resist this instant-gratification mindset. Plant, cultivate, and harvest. What you do today *does* matter.

Building Self-Discipline

One of the questions I often get about discipline is, "How can I build *more* self-discipline?" It's a great question and one I can answer very simply: **"Stop negotiating with yourself."**

If you say you are going to do something, commit to doing it, and do it. Period. Negotiating is a great skill in life and business, but it is a killer when it comes to self-discipline. So make it a rule to never negotiate with yourself.

Don't allow yourself to get caught up in a negotiation to sleep in just one extra hour, promising that tomorrow you will get up early and get after it. Don't negotiate to miss today's workout and work out twice as hard tomorrow. Don't put off today what you think can be done tomorrow.

Self-discipline is one of the most important ingredients of success at any level. The importance of having the ability to do what needs to be done cannot be overstated. This is a trait consistent in high performers. They simply don't negotiate with themselves.

You will not always *feel* like working out. You won't always *feel* like making your sales calls or responding to emails. But those things *need* to be done in order to achieve the outcome or reach the goal. And when the *feeling*—that thing most people call "motivation"—isn't present, that's when self-discipline becomes paramount.

CHAPTER SIX:

MY FIRST HORSE RACE

I vividly remember my very first NFL game.

But despite how much I had improved, I was understandably nervous. Not only was it my first time playing a *real* game at the pro level, but I also had the added pressure of being a starter due to several injuries to veteran wide receivers. My receivers coach, George Stewart, sensing my anxiety, asked me a series of questions to put the situation into proper perspective.

"Is this field one hundred yards long?" he asked. "Is this the same ball we've been using in practice? Is it still ten yards for a first down? Are we going to run the same plays in this game that we've been running in practice?"

The answer to all those questions was, "Yes!" And by asking me those questions, Coach Stew helped me realize that what I was about to do (play and start in my first NFL game) was no different and no more complex than what I had been doing for most of my life. It was still just football.

By putting this seemingly high-pressure, anxiety-filled situation into perspective, I was immediately able to relax, knowing I was prepared and capable of performing up to the levels of my ability. The "size" of the moment no longer affected me. Now, I *expected* to play well.

The Barnyard Forty

Back in the early summer of 1999, I was at Stockman's bar in Missoula, Montana. This was while I was at the University of Montana, but school was out for the summer. I had just come back from the Big Sky Conference track and field championships the day before.

If you've ever spent any time in Missoula, you've probably been to Stocks. Everybody goes to Stocks, and I spent my fair share of time there enjoying nights out with my teammates when I was college.

That night, I had stopped by Stock's to meet some friends and say hi to the owners of the bar (who were big Montana Grizzlies supporters), Mike and Donnie. We were making small talk, and Mike asked me how I had done in the track meet. I explained that I hadn't won, but I had performed well.

Right about then, a guy sitting at the bar who had clearly had few too many drinks asked, "You're a runner?"

"Yeah, I run track for the Griz," I said.

"You probably think you're pretty fast, huh?" this guy asked.

"Yeah, I'm pretty fast... I could beat you, if that's what you're asking!"

He then came back with an all-time classic line. He said, "Well, that may be, but I know someone I bet can smoke you in a race... my horse!"

Everyone at the bar within earshot burst out laughing. But, of course, being a cocky twenty-year-old college football player who had never even heard of a challenge I didn't like, I said, "Bring it."

The guy stared at me for a second, then said, "I bet you $500 that my horse can beat you over fifty yards."

Having fully devoted myself to improving my speed, I knew I possessed major competence in this area, so my confidence was through the roof. Still, I wasn't really sure what I was getting myself into. Not to mention that I was completely broke at the time. I certainly didn't have $500 to put up.

I didn't like the distance of fifty yards, either. I had grown up around horses, and I *knew* that horses typically don't start fast; they gradually get faster over longer distances. The shorter the distance, the better my chances. I was also taking into account that, as a football player, I had trained extensively to sprint forty yards at a time. My body was programmed to run that distance.

So I said, "All right. If you'll agree to do it over forty yards, you've got a deal."

We shook on it and agreed to meet at his ranch outside of Missoula the next day at noon.

I left the bar and immediately called my brother Dave, who was a team roper on the rodeo team at LC. "Bro," I said, "a guy just bet me $500 that his horse could beat me in a forty. I'm almost positive I can win. What do you think?"

My brother's response was, "Well, I don't know, but when was the last time you rode a horse?! Don't fall off!"

"No, I'm not riding a horse," I clarified. "I'm running, and *he's* riding a horse."

Dave thought about it for a second. "Well..." he said. "You run forties all the time, right? And you're fast in the forty. So, yeah, you should definitely win that."

That was all I needed to hear!

I showed up the next day with about ten of my teammates, partially hoping to find some strength and confidence in numbers, and partially to make sure there were some witnesses to this spectacle. I remember saying to someone on the way out there, "Talk about the Wild West... Only in Montana does a guy get himself into something like this."

As I warmed up and stretched a little, my opponent trotted out to the pasture on his horse, looking pretty smug as we got ready to get lined up. This was a first-class race; he had set up an old sprinkler head about forty yards down the pasture, and a two-by-four marked the starting line.

I looked at that sprinkler head, went through a quick visualization sequence, took a deep breath, got down in my three-point stance, and waited to hear the word "go."

When I heard it, I just exploded. My training took over, and I was in my own world for four and a half seconds.

I never saw the horse. It wasn't even close.

When I turned around, my teammates were standing there in amazement, and the guy on horseback couldn't believe what had just happened. They all thought they had just witnessed some amazing feat, but I had been confident all along that I would win. I was trained for the forty. My level of competence was extremely high. I was prepared for the moment, both physically and mentally. I was doing something I had done literally thousands of times before—although, granted, never in a pasture between a two-by-four and a sprinkler head.

Expect More

I know the anecdote in the previous pages might sound like some sort of small-town legend or tall tale, but it really happened. I raced a horse, and won. When I think back on that event, what's most crazy to me is that I actually *expected* to win.

In recent years, I have read numerous studies from the field of psychology around the topic of expectations. The theory is that one of the key contributors to unhappiness is disappointment. So, naturally, they recommend if you want to be happy, your best bet is to lower your expectations.

If all you want out of life is to be happy, then I would agree with this advice. But if you want to excel, stretch the limits of what is possible, and achieve true fulfillment, then I wholeheartedly disagree.

From the time I set that goal at age ten, through today, I maintain a practice of holding the highest possible expectations. I expect great things to happen. I expect to achieve anything I set out to do. I expect only the best from myself. I expected to win that race against a horse. And what I've found is that when you expect the best—more often than not—the best is exactly what you get. I expected to make every NFL team I tried out for, catch every ball thrown to me, and do my job perfectly on every play. Did those things happen every time? No. But more often than not, they did. When I retired from football and began in the speaking industry, I expected to be a great speaker and have success. When I sat down to begin writing this book, I expected it to be great.

Why hold such high expectations? Why NOT?! What is the alternative? Expect to be average or subpar, simply to avoid disappointment if things don't work out as well as you had hoped? You get out of life what you ask of it, so I will always ask for exactly what I want and expect to get it.

I once heard Tony Robbins tell a story about a homeless man who stopped him on the street and asked him for quarter. Tony reached in his pocket and pulled out some change, along with several hundred dollars in ten- and twenty-dollar bills, making sure the man saw the bills. He looked at the man and said, "Before

I give you this, I want to tell you something: life will give you what you ask of it." He handed the man the quarter and walked away.

The moral of the story is this: ask for MORE! Expect more...of yourself and from life. You may be surprised just how often *more* is exactly what you get.

CHAPTER SEVEN:

BE RELIABLE

Build confidence
Embody congruence
Finish what you started
Be coachable, humble,
proactive, and
resourceful

Reliable: consistently good in quality or performance; able to be trusted.

Over the course of six years in the NFL, I played for four organizations. No matter where I was or what team I was playing for, it was important to me that I was considered reliable—that my coaches could always trust me to show up and be ready to play well.

One of the tools I used to become more reliable was confidence. When we consider what makes a person reliable, confidence isn't typically the first quality that comes to mind, but in reality, **confidence and reliability are closely interconnected.** Let me explain.

Confidence comes in two main forms: 1) confidence we have in ourselves and our abilities and 2) the trust others have in us and our abilities.

Competence Creates Confidence

When we know we are good at something, or competent, we have a high degree of confidence in our ability to do that thing. As an example, I'll go back to the story of racing the horse. As a rational human being, I would have never even considered racing a horse, let alone believed I could win. But upon considering what the challenge truly really entailed—a forty-yard sprint—outrunning a horse went from seemingly impossible to something I felt extremely confident I could do.

I knew I was a competent sprinter, especially at forty yards. I knew I was trained and ready (track season had just finished, after all). And I knew all I had to do was rely on my skills and my training. The more I considered it, the more confident I became because I knew I was competent.

Think of how this concept may apply to you. A big challenge at work or in your personal life may seem insurmountable at first, but upon further examination, you may be surprised to discover that you possess more of the necessary skills than you think. If you don't, the first step is to become more competent.

The interesting thing about confidence is that it tends to be contagious. When you are confident in your abilities because you are competent, others become confident in you as well. For example, imagine for a moment you were diagnosed with a brain tumor and needed surgery to remove it immediately. What would give you confidence that the doctor performing the surgery can do the job extraordinarily well? The doctor's confidence in his or her abilities, of course! If you had a doctor who seemed uncertain about his or her skill level, you would likely feel anxious and uncertain about the surgery. If you had a doctor who assured you that they knew what they were doing, they had the skills to perform this surgery, and you would be OK, you would feel much better about undergoing the operation. Confidence and trust—reliability—are functions of each other.

When I'd first signed with the 49ers, I hadn't been a good punt returner. As you know from previous chapters, I failed miserably in my first audition, and it had quickly become evident that I was going to need to get better.

Starting that very next morning, I committed myself to catching one hundred punts per day. I got out to the practice field early, before most of my teammates, and practiced this specific skill over and over. Punt after punt.

I focused on different aspects every day. One day, it was my hand placement. The next day, it was my feet and making sure I had a good base and correct body placement. In a short period of time, I did get much better. I became more competent.

Before I knew it, I was practicing catching punts one-handed, behind my back, or with my vision impaired by a pair of "high tech" glasses modified with duct tape to cover one eye. As a result, my *confidence* as a punt returner increased in proportion to my competence. No longer did I get nervous during practice when we did punt return drills. I looked forward to it because I was good at it. As my competence and confidence levels increased, so did my reliability in the eyes of my coaches.

Pro-Level Reliability

In May of 2005, I was cut by the Falcons and signed by the Washington Redskins, now the Washington Football Team. This was an interesting time for the WFT organization. The year before, they had hired Joe Gibbs, who had previously coached the team to three Super Bowl championships and was already a member of the Pro Football Hall of Fame. He retired in 1992 and formed a NASCAR team, Joe Gibbs Racing, which has since won five NASCAR Cup Series championships. Dan Snyder, the team owner, was able to lure Gibbs out of retirement to coach the WFT from 2004 to 2007.

Joe Gibbs was a winner, pure and simple. I had heard a lot about what a great coach he was, and when I signed with the WFT, I was extremely excited to play for him. Initially, however, the prospects of me making that team did not look good.

The WFT already had a number of other great wide receivers. That meant it was a long shot that I would earn a spot on this team. But this was nothing new to me. *Everything* I had done up to that point had been a long shot, so I went about it the way I always did, which was to put my head down and get to work.

I began the process of proving to them that I was a smart, hardworking player they could count on. I also wanted to prove my versatility. There is an old saying in the NFL: "The more you can do, the more you can do." I took this notion to heart and put it to great use over the course of my career.

In this situation with the WFT, I determined that one way I could "do more" was to learn all the wide receiver positions in the offense, not just the position I primarily played. Typically, many players will only know their specific position. (If you are an X receiver, you only know the plays from the X position; if you're a Z receiver, same thing.) But I took it upon myself to learn *all* the wide receiver positions so I could play any one of them if I was ever needed.

Soon, I could play any position in the offense, and I spared no effort to prove myself to the coaches over the course of the spring and summer practices.

I also wanted to prove that I was hard worker in the weight room. Every team has a structured strength and conditioning program that they expect players to attend. Technically, they are voluntary, but for a guy like me, fighting to make the team, I considered them mandatory. Most teams keep track of their individual players' summer workouts—how many workouts each player did, attendance records, and so forth—and that off-season, my workout attendance was scored at 115 percent. We were required to work out four times a week, but I went in on the off-day to get in an extra workout.

When training camp started in August, I was anxious to get going. Through the first few weeks, I was performing well in practice and turning some heads, but the deciding factor would be how well I would perform in our four preseason games. I played well in the first three preseason games, but it was in the final game of the preseason when everything I had been working for came full circle. I started the game playing at Z receiver, and the X receivers were not playing well at all. Coach Gibbs went to my receiver coach, Stan Hixon, and told him, "Put Farris in at X."

"He doesn't play X," said Stan. "He's a Z. We can't put him in at X."

Coach Gibbs said, "No, put him in. I trust him. He'll know what to do."

On our next offensive series, I went in at X and proceeded to have one of my best games as a pro, catching two touchdown passes in that game.

The next day was roster cutdowns. I was feeling good about my chances of making the team and felt as though I had done enough to earn a coveted spot. Later that afternoon, Coach Gibbs called me into his office to inform me that he was cutting me.

"I've got to cut you," he said. "We need some people at other positions. You're good enough to make this team, but right now, just from a numbers standpoint (NFL teams allow fifty-three players on their active roster), I need guys at other positions, so I have to cut you. But I want you on my team. You've proven to me that you can play for this team, so the first opportunity I get to bring you back, I'll do it.

"So, I need you to stay ready," he continued. "When you go back to Atlanta, stay in shape and be ready to go. Because I'm promising you I'm going to bring you back, will you promise me that you'll stay ready to go and ready to come in and play?"

"Yes," I said. "I'll do that."

I can't say I was thrilled about this turn of events, but I'd known going in that this was a long shot. Thanks to my extra efforts, I had earned Coach Gibbs' trust, and I trusted him that he would make good on his word.

I went home to Atlanta and immediately began working out with my personal trainer. We structured my workouts to mirror the team's weekly schedule so that I was staying mentally and physically engaged and prepared. Every week, I sat waiting for the phone to ring while continuing my preparation. After two long months, nine games into the season, Coach Gibbs finally called and said, "I've got some injuries. I have a spot for you. I told you I'd bring you back. I'm bringing you back. Are you ready to go?"

"Absolutely," I said. "I'm ready to go."

By then, I hadn't played any real football in over two months. They signed me on a Tuesday, and I practiced with the team

Wednesday, Thursday, and Friday in preparation for our game that Sunday against the Chargers. On Thursday or Friday of that week, one of the local beat writers asked Coach Gibbs, "Hey, Farris hasn't played all season and is probably going to have to play a lot on Sunday due to the injuries. Do you have any concerns about him being ready to go?"

"No," said Coach Gibbs. "I'm not worried about him at all. I trust him. He'll be ready to go."

I ended up playing forty plays in the game on Sunday. I didn't make any mental errors, and I was in shape physically. I caught one pass and played well overall.

I went on to finish that season and play parts of two more seasons with the WFT under Coach Gibbs. Football aside, he taught me a valuable lesson about trust that has remained a core principle for me ever since—be reliable.

Coach Gibbs trusted that I'd be ready to go and that when the time came, all he'd need to do was call me, and I would not only show up but **show up ready to do the job, and more importantly, do it well.**

Likewise, my trust in *him* is the reason I stayed in shape. If I thought he wouldn't keep his word and re-sign me to the team, I wouldn't have done it. It was this mutual trust that we had in each other that made all the difference.

That experience really taught me the value of being reliable—of being someone other people could count on and trust. This was a trait I'd been practicing in my personal and professional life for years, largely unconsciously, but it was at that moment that I realized it was a hallmark of who I was as a player; it wasn't until that point that I realized whatever I lacked in skill or production, I made up for in reliability. All these years, coaches had been seeing that in me, and a part of my success was due to the fact that they knew I was a guy they could trust. That trait is one of the things that kept me in the NFL.

The more time passes, the more I come to realize the importance of that experience with Coach Gibbs. We both knew we could count on one another to be reliable. It's a powerful thing when trust and reliability can be reciprocated.

Reliability Vs. Dependability

Note that reliability differs from dependability. There seems to be a fundamental misunderstanding here.

Being dependable means that people can count on you to *show up*. You've no doubt heard the phrase "showing up is half the battle." I couldn't disagree more. Showing up is the prerequisite, but it's *none* of the battle. You get no applause for just showing up. Now, don't get me wrong, you do *have* to show up! But the battle begins *after* you show up and it's what you do at that point that really matters. Being reliable means you not only show up every time, but you show up, bring your best, and do your job exceptionally *well* every time.

Dependable people are a dime a dozen. You can hire just about anybody to get something done. As long as someone shows up, is safe, and reasonably smart, you can hire them to babysit your kids, for example. But wouldn't you want to feel as though you can trust that person to do the job extremely *well* to ensure that your children are safe and cared for to the highest degree possible? In this case, dependable just doesn't cut it. Anyone can sit in your house and watch your kids for a few bucks on a Friday night. But you want the babysitter who goes above and beyond. That's the difference. That's reliability.

Close the Loops—Finish What You Started

Another core characteristic of reliable people is the ability to keep and deliver on promises they make. Reliable people do what they say they are going to do and deliver on commitments. Put another way, if you are a reliable person, you are somebody who will finish what you start.

When I talk about this in my seminars, I ask, "How many times have you told somebody that you'd get something done for them, and you didn't deliver? How many projects have you started that you didn't complete?"

A funny example I tend to use is the never-ending bathroom renovation. You know, that bathroom that has been under reconstruction for two years. (If you can't relate to this personally, I bet you've at least been in a house at one point where this was the case.) This sort of bathroom seems to be in a perpetual state of remodeling. The owners started the project, tore down the old fixtures, and got new tile laid but still don't have the tub done, they haven't finished the sink, and the walls still need to be painted. The thought, of course, is that someday, they'll have enough time to finish it. But until then, their bathroom remains a wreck.

Many people live their whole lives with their bathrooms unfinished, so to speak. Every day, they are surrounded by projects they started but haven't completed. It could be a home improvement project or a business idea, but maybe it's something simpler, like a promise you made to your kids that you didn't follow through on, a conversation you started with a loved one or a significant other that you didn't finish, or the New Year's resolution that only lasted a month.

All these unfinished projects are what we call **open loops**. They are like tabs on your browser, sitting there idle, opened but not completed or finished. All they serve to do is take up bandwidth—mental and emotional energy.

In other words, open loops weigh us down and make us feel bad about ourselves because they serve as reminders of all our broken promises, incomplete projects, and unfinished checklists. Over time, this takes a serious toll on your mindset.

This may sound harsh, but if you think about how we look at people who live their lives with their literal and/or metaphorical bathrooms constantly unfinished, we don't trust them. And deep down, they don't trust themselves, either. All we have to do is look around to see that they don't follow through on things—they don't close the loop. If somebody continually disappoints us (and themselves) by failing to close the loops in their lives, then we can't trust them or see them as a reliable person.

A key trait of reliability is being somebody who finishes what you start. Do what you say you will do and keep the promises you make. Close those loops.

The good news is that closing open loops is easy to do. It as simple as taking action.

Congruence

It's one thing to *say* that you're a person who's reliable, committed, dedicated, and trustworthy. To back these claims up is something else entirely.

Congruence is when **your actions and your behaviors match up with who you say you are**. The two are in harmony. It's about walking the walk, not just talking the talk. If I show up and tell you I am a hard worker, but then you see me skipping days of work or giving half-hearted effort in workouts or neglecting my studies—or failing to do any of the things a *real* pro would be doing—then my actions are incongruent with who I told you I am.

In his book *The Charge: Activating the Ten Human Drives that Make You Feel Alive,* author and high-performance coach Brendon Burchard describes congruence as "how we think of ourselves (our self-image) and how we behave in accordance with that image in the real world." He goes on to say, "It's one of the most profoundly powerful drives we have as humans—to live in consistent alignment with who we think we are, how we want others to perceive us, and who we want to become."

And again, it's impossible to be someone who is reliable if your actions are consistently at odds with who you say you are and who you want people to believe you are.

Going back to my story with Coach Gibbs, I presented myself to the organization as a player they could count on. "I'm smart. I do my job. I do it well." But I didn't just *say* these things. Throughout the course of the off-season, my actions validated my words. And because my coaches saw the evidence in my actions and behaviors, they were able to say, "Yeah, Farris is just as he advertised. Everything he said about himself, and everything the Falcons coaches said about him, is true."

Congruence, therefore, is an extension of reliability. You can't be reliable unless you're also congruent. Your actions and your behaviors have to be in line with who you tell people you are or who you're presenting yourself to be. And only if that is the case will they trust you and see you as somebody who is reliable.

CHAPTER EIGHT:

MODELING EXCELLENCE

Earlier in this book, I described my first few practices with the 49ers and how I failed so miserably to make a good first impression. Luckily, I immediately realized there was no one to blame but myself. Putting myself at cause, admitting that I was the problem, empowered me to also be the solution. With this mindset, I was quickly able to find ways to improve and be more reliable, to myself and the coaches, using a method called modeling excellence. Finding a mentor, or someone who is having the level of success you desire, in your field of interest and modeling their actions is the quickest way to improve. You can bypass months or years of trial and error by learning from someone who has already walked the path you're walking.

This concept is one I learned as young child from my very first role model, my dad.

The summer before my sophomore year of high school, my dad got a car for my brother and me. We had both recently gotten our driver's licenses and would need a car to get to school, practices, and other activities. That summer, Dad asked me, "Are you going to get a job so you have some money for gas and hanging out with your friends?" I explained to my dad that I didn't want to get a job because I wanted to spend the summer focusing on working out and preparing myself for the upcoming football season.

This was a big deal because my dad *always* had a summer job—even as an adult. He was a teacher (later a school principal) and couldn't afford to take summers off and still be able to support his five children. So, during the summers of the 80s and early 90s, my dad worked twelve-hour days for a local company called Twin City Foods, walking for miles in the pea fields. Dad's job, every day from 6:00 a.m. to 6:00 p.m., was to patrol hundreds of acres of pea fields beneath the summer sun, looking for bugs on the crops so the company could determine what types of pesticides were needed for the plants.

Looking back on it now, it must have been a miserable job. I don't know *how* he did it. I only know *why*. Dad walked the pea fields all summer long, in the heat of Lewiston, Idaho, because he had a family to take care of.

When I was a kid, I wasn't always understanding or sympathetic to how tired he must have been after those twelve-hour days. As soon as he got home around 6:00 p.m., he would immediately load up and go to one of my baseball games or throw me footballs so I could practice my wide receiver skills in the backyard.

You hear a lot of high performers talk about heart-to-heart conversations with their fathers about how nobody was going to give them anything—how if you wanted something, you had to work hard for it. My dad never said that to me. He just lived it. And that became my model of the world.

My parents never spoke to me explicitly about hard work and dedication. They never sat me down for a lecture about doing what it takes to be successful. My parents weren't the type to lecture about those kinds of things; they just lived it, and I got those lessons through watching them do it. Hard work was ingrained in me at an early age. When I told my dad I wanted to focus on my workouts instead of getting a summer job, we *both* knew it wasn't because I was trying to avoid hard work. I had already learned what it meant to work hard from a great role model.

"Well, if you're going to focus on your workouts and be committed to that, then that's fine," said Dad. "I'll give you a couple bucks here and there when I can. You can pay me back by getting your college paid for."

And thanks to a football scholarship—earned from my commitment to all those workouts—that's what I did.

To this day, my dad is the most reliable person I know. I have gone to him numerous times as adult for help, advice, comfort, or a solution to a problem I was facing. If he didn't immediately have the solution, he found a way to provide it. He never lectures or belittles, and he takes the initiative to find multiple possible solutions. Through his actions he demonstrates resourcefulness, humility, and a proactive approach to problem-solving—traits that anyone aspiring to be great should strive to emulate.

The Core Four

The concept of modeling excellence is well known but, surprisingly, not often practiced. One reason for this is that many people simply aren't sure how to do it. In fact, when I introduce this idea in a coaching session or in a seminar, "How do I do it?" is often the first question that gets asked. So I want to take a minute here to address this question and give you the tools to help you implement this concept.

To help you successfully model excellence, I need to remind you of something we discussed back in Chapter 4. We talked about Clarity of Person—the idea of first focusing on who you need to be, rather than what you need to do. That applies here as well. Successfully modeling excellence will require you to *be* humble, coachable, resourceful, and proactive—something I call the Core Four.

If you remember, I described what it was like to be in the San Francisco 49ers locker room for the first time and see All-Pro wide receiver Terrell Owens walk in—and to suddenly realize that this superhero-like individual was my *teammate*. This superstar was the guy *I* now needed to be like.

I knew this opportunity with the 49ers might be my one and only shot to make it in the NFL. I needed to be the best I'd ever been at that moment. I needed to play at a level higher than I'd ever played before. I needed to grow instantly. I didn't have time to *get* better. If I was going to gain the trust of the coaches, I needed to *be* better...now!

I made a simple calculation: *Terrell Owens is the best, so if I do everything exactly the way T.O. does, to the best of my ability, I will be better!*

On the practice field, I observed T.O.'s every move and did my best to imitate or "model" his actions. I watched how he ran routes and caught the ball, and then imagined myself looking just like just him when it was my turn. After practice, if he lifted weights or sat in an ice bath, so did I. Whatever he ate for lunch, I ate. I was engaging in the process of **modeling excellence**, and it worked. No, I didn't become a Terrell Owens clone, but I did become a *much* better version of myself as a football player. I had chosen him as a role model and successfully modeled the habits, traits, and characteristics of an All-Pro.

Looking back, I can see that with that one action, I fulfilled all four criteria of being humble, coachable, resourceful, and proactive.

I was humble enough to know I needed to be a lot better than I was, and I couldn't do it on my own. People who are willing to humble themselves and admit that there's always more to learn and room to grow will have more success than those who believe they already know it all.

I was coachable because I was willing to learn more, listen to my mentors and coaches, and actually do what they suggested. In football, as in life, it's difficult to trust people who aren't coachable. People who aren't willing to do what they are being taught or asked to do simply aren't reliable when it comes time to get the job done.

I was resourceful in asking myself the question, "How am I going to get better?" And then finding the answer: "Act like that guy!" When I was unsure of exactly to do to get better, I found someone that could help me—someone to emulate. People will often claim that the reason they can't get something done or why they failed was because they didn't have the resources. To me, the most valuable resource is resourcefulness itself—being able to get the job done in spite of not having the resources. Coach Gibbs, for example, didn't send a coach to monitor me or a trainer to help me work out. I did all that on my own. If you have enough passion, determination, energy, and commitment, you can always find the resources you need. That is what it means to be resourceful. Those who need the answers served up on a silver platter can't be trusted to get it done.

And finally, I was proactive because I saw what I needed to do, and I went after it. I didn't wait for somebody to tell me to do it. Right, wrong, or somewhere in between, my course of action was attaching myself at Terrell's hip and doing everything he did, exactly the way he did it, and hoping that would be the key to getting better. I made the decision that this was what needed to be done, and I went in and did it myself. Just like my dad in the pea fields, I saw that there was work that needed to be done, so I buckled down and did it.

I use this example to illustrate how powerful of a tool modeling excellence can be in helping you become more reliable, and how exercising the Core Four—humility, coachability, resourcefulness, and proactivity—is the key to doing it successfully.

CHAPTER NINE:

BE OBSESSED

Abandon rationality
Narrow your focus
Relentlessly search for
wisdom and mentors
Refuse to consider
another outcome

Obsessed: to preoccupy the mind (of a person) excessively.

Earlier in this book, I shared the story of Head Coach Mick Dennehy at the University of Montana telling me I wasn't fast enough to play with the big boys. In Chapter 3, I mentioned that I had worked hard to get faster and prove I had what it took.

Well, the truth is, I did a little more than just "work hard" to get faster. Even after making it to the University of Montana and proving I had what it took to play at the college level, I never forgot the words of Mick Dennehy.

"We just don't think you're fast enough to really make a difference at our level."

I became *obsessed* with proving Coach Dennehy wrong.

When I reported to camp in Montana in the fall of my freshman year, it was clear that I wouldn't be playing that season. I would be redshirting, which meant that I was on the team and went to all the practices but couldn't play in any games as a freshman. Many college programs around the country redshirt a majority of their freshman players to give them an extra year to grow and mature personally and improve as players. I saw this as a good thing for me and used the year exactly as it was intended.

Every day during the season, I would work out in the morning with all the other freshman redshirts, then go practice in the afternoon and stay for the meetings after practice, which lasted until about 6:00 p.m. or 6:30 p.m. After that, we would go to dinner, followed by study hall every night until 9:00 p.m. But I still wasn't done.

In keeping with my obsession to improve my speed, I found a way to get in an extra, somewhat secret, workout after study hall.

Rational Thinking No Longer Applies

On the backside of the old fieldhouse at the University of Montana was a scarcely used door that would become one of my greatest assets. It became my "secret" access to the fieldhouse, which would typically be locked and closed for the night by the time I was looking to get in this extra workout. In order gain entry after hours, I put a little piece of athletic tape over the lock of that door before I left for dinner so that when the door was closed, the latch couldn't extend to lock the door. To any observer, the door looked closed and presumably locked. And because it was rarely, if ever, used, I was confident no one would ever check.

After my study hall, at about 9:30 p.m., I would go back to the fieldhouse, through that door, and descend the stairs down onto the basketball court.

With the bleachers surrounding the court retracted, as they usually were when there wasn't a game being played, I could use the fifty or sixty yards of rubberized surface alongside the court to run sprints and do various drills the university track coach had given to me.

With the lights off after hours, the only light illuminating the surface was the red glow of the Exit signs on either end of the arena. They didn't emit much light, but they lit up the surroundings enough for me to see what I was doing.

So there in the closed field house, after hours, in private, I would run sprints and do a series of drills to work on my speed secretly, when nobody was watching.

I did this three nights a week throughout the season that first fall, and then continued when I came back to campus after Christmas break, all the way through January, February, and March. I continued doing these sprint workouts on my own because I was totally obsessed with improving my speed and dispelling this idea that I wasn't fast enough. I would soon get my chance.

In March of every year, we did what was called spring testing to cap off six to eight weeks of winter workouts. The testing was comprised of lifting and sprinting, among other fitness and endurance tests, and one of the tests was obviously the forty-yard dash, which is what I had been preparing for.

Even though they had already given me a scholarship and I was already on the team, I still wanted to prove the coaches wrong and change their opinions of me.

To make it competitive, we ran the forty in pairs, two guys at a time. The idea was that the race-like conditions would cause both guys to run faster. I had my eye on a kid named David Gilbreath, who had been the 100m and 200m state champion in Montana. He was also one of the players they had chosen to offer a scholarship ahead of me. I specifically remember Mick Dennehy telling me, "We're going to offer a scholarship to this kid over you because he's the state 100-meter champion. He's an explosive player."

Naturally, he was the one I wanted to race against.

When it came time to run forties, we were divided into two single-file lines. I was third or fourth in line when I quickly realized that Gilbreath was next up to run in the lane next to me. I wasted no time and cut the line to get in front of a few of my teammates so I could challenge Gilbreath. When my teammates saw what was happening, they got into the competitive spirit. What seemed like the whole team got out of line and lined up down the sides of the track. The atmosphere was, "Okay, this isn't a drill. This is for real."

We raced "for real" that day, and I smoked him. It wasn't even close.

As I was walking back to get in line to run another one, I walked past Coach Dennehy and said, "Am I fast enough now?"

Mick smiled, presumably remembering our conversation from the previous year, and said, "Yeah. I think that'll work."

Not only did I beat Gilbreath; my time that day was the fastest forty-yard dash time on the entire team. My hard work had paid off.

I don't tell this story to brag. I tell it to introduce the concept of obsession. Because that is what it took for me to improve my speed and achieve countless other big goals throughout the course of my life: **absolute obsession.**

The truth is, Mick Dennehy had been right. I *wasn't* fast enough to have outrun the Montana State 100-meter champion back when he'd passed on me in favor of faster players. But I became obsessed with changing that reality, and obsession is what fueled me to do whatever it took to get faster.

In retrospect, when I consider what I was willing to do to make this happen, it was **completely irrational.** Sneaking into the field house after hours to get these workouts in—usually my third workout of the day—was nuts. This was not normal behavior! Rational thinking was totally out the window. But it was necessary, so I did it.

As I said earlier, success comes with a price, and you have to be willing to pay that price day in and day out.

Singular Focus

The issue of **focus** comes up quite frequently with average-level performers. They say they want to get better and will focus on four or five different areas where they want to improve. In other words, they are spreading themselves too thin.

The ancient Latin writer Publilius Syrus once wrote, "To do two things at once is to do neither." If you want to be your best, make real change, get real results, and you are obsessed about what you're doing, **your focus must be narrow, singular, and laser-like on a specific target.** Only after you have reached a new level of competency or met your desired outcome can you shift focus to another target.

As a teenager, all I would talk about was football. All my time was spent training for football. My focus was narrow...singular. Sure, I was playing basketball and running track, and although I enjoyed those things, the real reason I was doing them was to become a better football player. Track was to get faster. Basketball was to improve my body control and to become more agile, more athletic, and more explosive.

People used to say I had blinders on—that football was all I thought about, day and night. They were absolutely right. I took it as a compliment.

As I got older and began spending more time around world-class athletes—and, later, when I retired from football and spent time around world-class CEOs and leaders in business—I realized that singular focus was a trait common among all of them.

In the book *Outliers*, author Malcolm Gladwell outlines a concept known as the "10,000 hours" rule. The theory is that 10,000 hours is the approximate amount of time required to become a master of any given pursuit. Study the lives of the so-called prodigies and geniuses who have achieved phenomenal success, and you'll find that they were outliers who wisely leveraged every advantage available and committed to literally thousands of hours practicing their skills and honing their crafts.

Gladwell estimates that the Beatles put in 10,000 hours of practice playing in Hamburg, Germany in the early 1960s and that Bill Gates put in well in excess of 10,000 hours of programming work before founding Microsoft. For the Beatles, a unique setup in the Hamburg nightclub scene allowed them to play longer sets than most bands, thus allowing them to accumulate their 10,000 hours more quickly than most bands. And Bill Gates, who enjoyed otherwise unheard-of access to a computer lab at the University of Washington while he was just a teenager, gave up everything else to spend fifteen to sixteen hours a day coding. While his friends were at the beach or out acting their age, Gates was focused on what he said he wanted, building up his 10,000 hours. It may sound crazy, but it takes that level of obsessive, singular focus to achieve something big.

In Mark Cuban's book, *How to Win at the Sport of Business: If I Can Do It, You Can Do It*, he shares how, in his twenties, he was sharing a living space with five or six other people while trying to get his company off the ground. He didn't do anything other than work at that business, work towards the goal that he set for himself. He, like other high performers, had devoted himself to a singular purpose and was obsessed with it.

If you just want average results, then no problem, but to be the best and take it over the top, you have to have a laser focus in a specific area.

Relentlessly Searching for Wisdom and Mentors

If you spend any time around highly successful people and uber-high performers, you will see two things.

Number one: They **know their role models** off the tops of their heads and can name their mentors. They all have somebody after whom they modeled themselves, someone who served as their mentor early in their career and may still be their mentor.

Number two: They are **continuously improving themselves**. No matter what level of success they have achieved—billionaire, multi-billionaire, founder of a Fortune 100 company—they are consuming most of the material on the personal-development market. These are people who are constantly going to seminars, reading books, seeking wisdom around their field or passion, and searching for ways to do what they do better.

When I met Terrell Owens, he was already one of the best players in the NFL. But he was still constantly looking for an edge—a new trainer, massage therapist, or sports therapist who could help him be 1 percent better, or even half a percent better.

I remember one time when Terrell and I pulled out a ten-year-old practice film of Jerry Rice, who was probably considered the greatest receiver of all time, just to watch him in practice and see if we could pick up on any small nuances in the way he ran a particular route or used certain techniques to get open. Terrell and I were obsessed—searching for anything that might help us get better. High performers, even when they're at the top of their game, are still seeking knowledge and wisdom wherever they can find it. It doesn't matter if the whole world thinks they're the greatest at what they do; they're trying to become the best possible version of *themselves*.

The consistent, relentless pursuit of wisdom and mentors is a key trait, habit, or behavior of all super-high-performing people.

Unwilling to Consider Another Outcome

I used to despise when people would ask me, "So, what's your backup plan? If football doesn't work out, do you have something to fall back on?"

Absolutely not.

I had no backup plan. There was nothing to fall back on because I was 100 percent focused on making Plan A work. Every minute or second that I spent thinking about Plan B was time that I could have been focused on Plan A—wasted time, in other words. Obsession, to me, means **there is no Plan B**.

If you're married, you'll understand what I mean. What if, on your wedding day, you had said, "Well, I have to have a Plan B ready in case this doesn't work out." Not a good start to a marriage! No, you are 100 percent focused on making that one relationship, Plan A, the best that it can be. There's no Plan B in marriage, and there shouldn't be in life, either.

Until Plan A doesn't work, high performers remain focused on Plan A. And if Plan A doesn't work, if that business fails or that lifelong dream never comes to fruition despite our best efforts...

fine. We go to a new Plan A (more on this in the next chapter). But this idea of being unwilling to consider another outcome—unwilling to consider the possibility that what you're going for, what you're striving for, won't work—that's the obsessive mind. That's what causes you to put in those extra hours to be more prepared, more reliable, and more obsessed. That's what allows you to elevate yourself to be the best version of yourself and reach the world-class levels of a true pro.

In January of 2020, I stepped on the scale in bathroom and was surprised to see that I weighed around 215 pounds. My NFL playing weight had been between 196 to 198 pounds. In the ten years since retiring, I continued to work out and stay in decent shape, but I had gotten to a point where I no longer liked the way I looked and wanted to make some changes.

Most people would have looked at me and said I was in good shape, but I was carrying more body fat than I would have liked. What I really wanted was to get my "football body" back—lean, sleek, and muscular—and what I'd been doing up to that point clearly hadn't worked. I decided to follow the ketogenic diet. As a full-blown sugarholic, I knew it would be difficult, but I was up for the challenge and committed to being "all-in." I cut all sugar and nearly all carbohydrates out of my diet, cold turkey. That's my personality. If I go all in, I'm all in.

In six weeks, I had lost 20 pounds and was back down to 195. What surprised me the most was that I was able to lose the weight *without* working out. Once the excess body fat was gone, I started lifting weights again to put some muscle back on. Now, I am arguably in better shape at forty-three years old than I was at twenty-three years old.

Was it easy? No. But I decided that I was going to get the body I wanted and wouldn't accept anything less.

I think this story illustrates not only the idea of being unwilling to consider another outcome but also many of the elements of preparation that were discussed in Chapter 4. I had *Clarity of Purpose* (lose 20 pounds and get my football body back), *Clarity of Person*, or who I would need to become (a healthier eater) in order to achieve the goal, and finally, *Clarity of Plan* (the keto diet), which, if followed correctly, would deliver the results I wanted.

While I still crave many of my old favorite foods and will occasionally indulge in pizza, burgers, and ice cream, I've made the commitment to myself to prioritize my health and fitness.

The best part is that, once again, I proved to myself that if I simply follow a blueprint, I can achieve the goals I set and make lasting change in any area of life I chose.

What's disappointing is the number of people I talk to who have taken similar measures that will say, "I did that too. I lost thirty pounds. I was feeling great and loving the way I looked, but then I fell off the wagon and gained all the weight back."

It's tragic how many people will reminisce about a time in their life when they were successful at something. They know what to do—they've done it before! But they are no longer doing what they know works. They look in the mirror, they look at their life, and they know that this isn't where they want to be. They know how to change it; they're just no longer doing what it takes.

One reason I believe this happens is because now, more than ever, we are living in an instant-gratification society. Even when we see results quickly, and make progress, the commitment necessary to maintain those results over the long-term, and ultimately reach the goal, is just too difficult. Obsessive, singular focus and the unwillingness to consider another outcome means delaying instant gratification in favor of the long-term benefit.

Hyperbolic Discounting

If I were to offer you $10 today or $20 three months from now, which would you choose?

Now, I can't think of many investments that will guarantee you'll double your money three months, but it's been shown that most people will opt for $10 today. Even though $20 is double the money, the value of the $20 tends to get discounted in their minds based on the length of time before they can get it. Most people will take the immediate reward right now, which is of lesser value, over waiting for the bigger reward. Three months is just too long.

This is known as hyperbolic discounting, a behavioral economics concept that suggests people are prone to choose smaller, immediate rewards over larger, later rewards. The point is, if you are clean on your diet and you work out every day, in three months or six months, you will see the change. You know you'll see a change. You are, in fact, guaranteed to see a change. But, although most of us would love to have that body, it's six months in the future (a greater, delayed reward), while that cupcake or piece of pizza is in front of our faces *right now*. The instant reward is, in most people's minds, of greater value than the long-term reward.

This concept also applies to procrastination. When you procrastinate, you are choosing the instant gratification of enjoying some free time, rather than the future reward of working on or completing the project or assignment that's due next week.

Small Targets, Big Goals

Hyperbolic discounting is one possible explanation for why so many people in America today have no retirement plan and no savings. Although we know the future reward of retiring with several million dollars will be extremely comforting and satisfying, the immediate joy of buying that shiny new boat so the family can enjoy weekends on the lake holds more value in the moment. The concept of delayed gratification has been lost in our instant-gratification society, with instant access to everything and no shortage of welcome distractions.

I get it. You want the instant gratification of being able to take your family out on the boat every weekend or take that trip to Vegas with your buddies. But what is the true cost of those things in the long run? If those rewards in the short term are jeopardizing your future goals or plans, is it really worth it?

One of the things I teach in my seminars is a process of setting the big goal (which might be setting up a retirement account, building up some savings, or losing fifty pounds) and then setting small targets along the way. Set a goal to save x amount of dollars over the next several months. If you hit the goal, reward yourself with an *inexpensive* trip to Vegas. If the big goal is to lose fifty pounds, that might take you a year to achieve. Set a target to lose four pounds a month and celebrate that achievement by having a few beers with your friends, or a wine night with your girls. This mitigates the damage of hyperbolic discounting by allowing you to hit a short-term target and celebrating that. You feel like you are getting a reward in the short term, which satisfies your need for instant gratification while also moving you towards the big goal.

CHAPTER TEN:

A NEW "PLAN A"

In the previous chapter, I shared the importance of obsession and singular focus—of cultivating a mindset of being 100 percent focused on Plan A, devoting all my time and energy to making a Plan A work.

But you may now be asking yourself, what if Plan A doesn't work?

What if, despite doing everything right, I hadn't made it into the NFL? What if, after devoting myself singularly to my vision, I fell short? What happens when Plan A goes wrong?

To this day, I make it a point to never have a Plan B to fall back on. If and when it becomes apparent that Plan A isn't sustainable, my mindset has always been to fall *forward* into a new Plan A.

There's no fallback plan. There's no plan of retreat. Only a plan forward.

This may seem like an arbitrary distinction, but it all comes back to the mental game. The idea of **having something to fall back on gives people an out**. It's one of the things that contributes to people quitting when they are so close to the breakthrough. Having an exit plan takes you out of that back-against-the-wall, got-to-do-everything-I-can-to-make-this-work-because-I-don't-have-a-fallback-plan mindset.

That mindset is key. If you're going to make something big happen, you can't have any other mindset. If you want to take the island, you've got to burn your boats.

Make it work. It's got to.

Failure Is Feedback

Anybody who's ever done anything great has experienced multiple failures along the way. In other words, their Plan A didn't work. Don't be surprised when it happens to you. It's supposed to. It may not feel like it at the time, but failure is something you should look at in a positive light.

I was taught early in my athletic career to see failure or slip-ups as feedback. They provide useful information about the areas we can improve, get better, and increase the likelihood we will get it right or have success next time.

The premise of a book called *Win or Learn: MMA, Conor McGregor and Me: A Trainer's Journey* by John Kavanagh is that you either win and get what you want, or you learn valuable lessons. In other words, every loss is just an opportunity to learn. This mindset is in alignment with how I tend to think about failure: in the context of **preserving the things you've learned and reframing them.** It's all about your perspective.

Kobe Bryant was once asked how he felt about losing. He said, "I don't like to lose, but once I've lost, I embrace it because it's an opportunity to grow and get better and see where we made mistakes and where we could do things better. How you really grow is by getting the feedback from a loss or a failure." Again, it comes down to mindset and discipline.

It's a simple choice. Is your failure going to defeat you, or are you going to learn from it and keep moving forward?

You either give up, or you say, "No, that's not going to be the last chapter of this book. I'm going back in." That's the difference between amateurs and pros. The people who ultimately succeed just keep going.

Some years ago, I attended a conference where the speaker asked, "What do you think the chances are that I can flip a coin and make it land heads up ten times in a row?" As you might expect, people in the audience responded that the chances were very slim. Ten times in a row, heads? But his theory was that the chance that he could do it was 100 percent. Why? Because he wasn't going to stop until it happened. With an infinite number of chances, at some point, even if the odds are just .001 percent, success becomes inevitable. The speaker assured us he would flip that coin until he reached that .001 percent result.

In most things, you ultimately have as many chances as you want. You can flip the coin as many times as you like—take as many swings at the plate as you desire. It's up to you to decide at what point you exit the game and say you failed and it didn't work.

CHAPTER ELEVEN:

THE RESET

Being a football player was all I ever wanted to be. And I went for it with every ounce of my being. I maxed out every ounce of talent and ability I was given. Every time it appeared as though I had hit the ceiling of what was possible, I punched through and went higher.

That being said, I was never the best player in the NFL or even the best on my team. But I was always striving to be the very best player *I* could be. Could I have done more and been even better? Maybe. But I'm content knowing that I consistently asked myself that question—"How can I be the best version of myself?"—and put in the work necessary to answer it. I proved to myself that anything I truly wanted to do, I could do it.

And that is why I was so disgusted with the man I saw in the mirror that day back in January of 2013. I wasn't being honest with myself.

I had new goals and things I wanted to accomplish, but I wasn't *doing* any of the things I had done to climb that first mountain. I wasn't applying the blueprint—be prepared, be reliable, and be obsessed. The habits, the work ethic, the commitment, and the dedication were gone. How could I expect to have any success climbing the next mountain? I was no longer following the plan.

The way I was living was contradictory to everything I had done in the past—everything I believed to be true. I had a system that I had developed and used to achieve every goal I'd set in life, and it had worked. I'd achieved my childhood dream by using this blueprint. I couldn't tell you at what point I'd decided I didn't need a blueprint anymore, but I now knew I'd been dead wrong.

I made the decision, at that moment, to change. To apply the blueprint to my current goals and dreams and implement those habits and create an even better version of me.

I started with the basics, just as I had many years ago as a kid. I got up an hour earlier and began a morning routine consisting of reading, journaling, and working out. I bought a daily planner so I could plan my days, weeks, and months. I wasn't winging it anymore...I was *preparing*. I started a new workout plan, a blueprint to follow, to avoid just going to the gym and going through the motions as I had been doing for the past several years. I broke my big goals down into smaller targets and began tracking my progress. I cleaned up my diet to help shed a few extra pounds but also to begin to re-instill the discipline I once had. Because I was staying committed to the small things, I started to trust myself more and became more *reliable* to myself. I started to believe again that I was capable of doing something great. My self-confidence began to return, and I started taking risks again and getting outside of my comfort zone. In a short time, some interesting things began to happen. I started to see opportunities—ones that had presumably been there all along but I had yet to see. Doors that I wasn't even aware of began to open.

My Next Thing

One evening, I was flying standby out of Atlanta Hartsfield Jackson Airport on a buddy pass provided to me by a friend who was an employee of the airline. It must have been my lucky day because I was assigned a seat in first class, something that rarely happens to a standby passenger.

I settled into my seat and began making small talk with the gentleman sitting to my right.

"Is Atlanta home?" I asked.

"No, San Francisco. I've been here all week on business, and I'm headed home now."

He proceeded to tell me was VP of sales for a large company in the financial services industry and had been in Atlanta for their annual conference.

He proceeded to ask me a question I'd come to dread over the past several years. "What do you do?"

I hated that question because I didn't have a good answer for it. At that time, I was three years removed from my NFL career and hadn't yet found my next "thing."

The honest answer to his question was nothing. I didn't technically *do* anything. I had no job, no career, and no clue what I even wanted to pursue.

"I'm in what you might call early retirement," I said with a laugh. "I played pro football for a number of years, and now I'm kind of relaxing and seeing what's out there."

"You played pro ball?!" he asked excitedly. "That's awesome. How many people get to say that? It's like .0001 percent or something, right?"

"Something like that," I said with a smile.

"I played football for a year in college!"

"Oh, really?" I asked.

"Yeah, I was a walk on. I got my ass kicked for a year, decided I wasn't good enough, and that was it," he said as he laughed out loud.

"I miss it, though...I miss being an athlete. The mindset, mentality, discipline, commitment, accountability, truly working together as team...all of it. I've tried to bring some of that into my career now and instill some of it into my team, but it's hard. Most people just don't have that athlete's mindset. But I've often thought...if I could just get my team to have a little bit more of that mindset... to think like an athlete, and apply it to our industry, man, we could go to another level."

"I wish there was someone out there who could come in and teach it to my team," he continued. "I'd pay top dollar for that... the ROI would be huge."

I felt like someone had just slapped me across the face. *That's it.* If there was one thing I knew, it was the mindset of an athlete. I had spent two decades of my life as an athlete and competed at the highest level. I had a deep understanding of the mindset of world-class athletes and could surely teach it to others to help them raise their game in business, or any area of life, for that matter, the same way I had as a football player.

When our plane landed, he handed me his business card and told me to give him a ring if I was ever in the Bay Area.

"I'll do it," I said.

I never did. I lost the card and, to this day, cannot remember his name or the company he worked for. If I could remember, I would surely look him up and thank him for the gift he gave me that day.

Because of him and our conversation, I had found my next thing.

Immediately upon landing, I googled "motivational speaker training" and clicked on the first link that popped up, enrolled in the course, and began my speaking and coaching my career. I started studying the speakers whose styles I wanted to model. I spent thousands of dollars on public speaker training workshops and seminars, and I heard that old friend *obsession* calling my name once again. I read every business and self-help book I could get hands on and began to implement some of the principles into my life and teach them to others when and where I could. I started writing coaching and training programs, even though I didn't yet have any clients or anywhere to deliver them. I recorded myself giving speeches, critiqued my delivery, made notes, and went right back at it.

All told, it was several years before I booked my first speech and signed my first coaching client. Several years spent practicing, studying, learning, and honing my craft. It paid off. I knocked my first big speech out of the park. My first coaching client still works with me today. I've expanded to running workshops, seminars, and multi-day masterminds—training companies and individuals on the champion mindset of world-class athletes and high performers and teaching them how they can implement these principles into their own lives and businesses.

It is some of the most fulling work I've ever done, and it all happened because I went back to the basics and followed the blueprint. Sure, the goal was different, but the process was largely the same. Be prepared, reliable, and obsessed. Practice good habits. Stay disciplined, committed, and persistent. Do the simple, basic, ordinary things at an extraordinary level.

I truly believe this is the recipe to achieve any goal or dream, or take any area of your life to the next level. Is it the only way? Of course not. As I said in the introduction of this book, this is simply the best way that *I* know.

My hope is that you'll use this blueprint to get going. Follow the plan I've laid out, adopt and implement the habits of all pros (which you'll learn in the next section), gain some momentum, and see the results of the work you're putting in. Ultimately, however, I want you to develop you own blueprint, your own system, your own process. Something that's tailor made for you, by you. If you believe that being all-in and fully invested matters—and I believe strongly that it does—you'll never be more all-in on a plan than you will be when it's your own.

CHAPTER TWELVE:

THE FREEDOM TO DREAM BIG

Back in Chapter 2, I shared how I never felt any type of pressure from my parents to succeed. My parents' love, support, and acceptance were never conditional upon my success or who I became or whether I achieved my goals. They always encouraged me to go for it, and I never felt as if I would be disappointing them if I failed.

To this day, if I tell my parents of my new goals and ambitions—speaking at seminars and writing my first book—they support and encourage me unreservedly. And if I were unsuccessful, they would still welcome me with open arms. That's just the way my parents are.

That unconditional love and support is literally the thing that shaped me into the man I am today. If I want to do something, I just go for it. I feel the freedom to dream big. My motivation is internal rather than external because I have pursued the challenges that I truly cared about instead of searching for approval from my parents, family, friends, or doing things to please others.

This is my wish for you, moving forward—that you can have this same sort of internal drive to pursue your goals and dreams, removed from external, conditional love, support, or acceptance. Only you know what you truly want in life. I challenge you to find it and go for it with everything you've got!

Success Has Never Been Easier

Here is the best part: no matter what you're trying to achieve, many of the tools are already at your fingertips. In fact, you have fewer excuses now than you've ever had because you live in a time when you have unlimited access to information.

When I was a kid, I didn't have the internet. I couldn't go type in "drills to improve my speed" on YouTube and watch a video of you Usain Bolt, the fastest man in the world, doing sprint drills and mimic his workouts to improve my speed. I didn't have that at my disposal. All of my training was based off on what I thought would work, what someone I knew told me would work, or something I had read in a book.

No matter what your ambition may be, it is easier right now than it has ever been to grow, to learn, to get better, and to find the resources that can help you. Starting a business today versus starting a business thirty years ago is like night and day. You don't need a business degree from an Ivy League college. You can go online and literally Google "how to start a business" and find thousands of resources from experts on exactly how to do that— everything from how to raise capital to how to structure your LLC and anything else you might need to know. You can be, do, and have anything that you want. Hell, people are making millions of dollars posting pictures on Instagram. You have no excuse.

It has never been easier to take your life or your business to whatever level you want, but you still have to do the work. Part of the downside of the technology and the ease of information is that people have forgotten that just because you can find every-thing on demand now, it doesn't mean that success will happen overnight. Success happens over time, and we seem to have lost the value of time.

It takes time to perfect your craft. It took Jordan and Kobe and Tom Brady years—if not decades—to ultimately get to their level. Remember: plant, cultivate, harvest. All things in due time. But if you're determined and willing to put in the work, it's easier now than it's ever been to take your life or career to the next level and become the best version of yourself.

In addition to the information you constantly have at your fin-gertips, I have compiled the 33 Habits of All Pros in the next sec-tion of this book to further assist you. Turn the page to discover the simple things you can start doing today to get better and be your best.

PART II:

THE 33 HABITS OF ALL PROS

"People do not decide their futures. They decide their habits, and their habits decide their futures."
— F.M. Alexander

Deconstructing the High-Performance Myth

Throughout this part of the book, I will be sharing the 33 Habits of All Pros. These are the habits, characteristics, and traits common among all high performers. I have developed this list as a result of analyzing my own experiences—what worked for me and what hindered me in my career and personal experiences; working with top-tier athletes, business owners, and CEOs; observing the other pros that I had the privilege of working with in the NFL; and from the personal accounts of the great successes of the modern world.

At times, some of these habits will seem obvious. They may even appear redundant or, frankly, simple. This is intentional because the things you need to do to be your best and go to the next level are simple—but they are not necessarily easy.

Going from where you are to where you want to go will require that you adopt new habits and behaviors. I've heard it said that we don't get our goals; we get our habits. In other words, we don't get what we want, we get what we do and work for. Regardless of how badly we want to achieve a given goal, if our daily habits aren't congruent with what it takes, we are unlikely to ever realize it.

The point of sharing these 33 Habits is to deconstruct the myth that high performers are anomalies and outliers. They are not.

They are regular people taking regular actions extraordinarily well. It is that simple.

Many people feel LeBron James is an anomaly. And, yes, it's true that LeBron was born with that body. But there are plenty of six-foot-eight, 260-pound dudes walking around who didn't become professional basketball players. The only difference between them and LeBron James is that LeBron put in the work. He did things that they could be doing—the things they could have done that they chose not to do.

What follows are the habits I have identified as those core components that, if grasped successfully and implemented into your life, will separate you from the herd.

Each of the 33 Habits is presented with a set of Reflection Questions. I encourage you to keep a journal as you work through this section of the book. Answer the Reflection Questions thoughtfully and honestly, in as much detail as possible. This process isn't just about learning a few new strategies; it's about adopting a new way of thinking about success—committing to a high-performance mindset.

PROS HAVE WORLD-CLASS HABITS

You'll notice that I've chosen not to define the word "habit" up until this point. For most of us, it's pretty self-explanatory. Habits are nothing more than what we consciously or unconsciously do on a daily basis.

As such, your habits can be your best friends or your worst enemies. A high performer understands the importance of forming and sustaining the habits that ensure that they continually live up to their best, day in and day out. In essence, they make developing and practicing world-class habits, a habit.

The quality of your life and the height of your success is determined by the quality of your habits, and **reaching new levels of success is as simple as changing and upgrading your habits.**

Reflection Questions

1. What are three habits that, if integrated into your daily life, could improve your circumstances drastically?

2. Amateurs see habits as something to break—often because they are conscious of the negative habits that they have. What is one negative habit that you would like to give up for good?

PROS ARE HONEST

High performers are notorious for being brutally honest with others, but more importantly, they are brutally honest with themselves.

Average performers are often delusional about their skills and abilities. And while average performers are likely to claim that they're working much harder and putting in more time than they actually are, **pros live in objective reality**. This is to say that they are honest about their efforts, their skills, and their shortcomings.

The ability to see things as they truly are is what sets high achievers apart and gives them clarity on what is needed for them to grow, improve, and reach the next level.

Reflection Questions

1. Are you being honest with yourself about your skills, abilities, and level of competency? If not, in what ways have you been dishonest with yourself, and why do you think that is the case?

2. What are three things you could do to get better and take yourself to the next level in one area of your life?

PROS ARE DECISIVE

The ability to make quick decisions is a trait of nearly all high performers. Why? Because indecision leads to inaction, and inaction leads to stagnation.

While amateurs lack confidence in their ability to make sound judgments—and therefore, waste time deliberating on their decisions—**high performers are busy taking action** on the decision they made weeks ago. Do they *always* make the best possible decision? No. But they are willing to make tough decisions, in uncertain environments, and to accept responsibility for the outcome.

Many people are so concerned about the possibility of being wrong that they fail to act at all. The great thing about making a decision is that if you make the wrong one, you can simply make a new decision. This is called course-correction, and pros do it all the time. What's important is that you *make* a decision and then take subsequent action.

It won't be easy. I won't pretend that it will be. But when it comes to personal development and creating the best version of yourself, **ease is not the objective; growth is**. And there will no doubt be growing pains. Set your mind right now to embrace that.

Comfort is the enemy of growth. I've heard it said many times that to be great, you have to get uncomfortable. You have to force yourself outside of your comfort zone. So while I promise it won't be easy, I also promise it will absolutely be worth it.

Reflection Questions

1. In what ways have you allowed yourself to remain stuck in your comfort zone?

2. What is one big decision that you have been putting off? Why are you reluctant to take action?

PROS WELCOME ADVERSITY

Inside the weight room at my old high school was a poster that read, "Adversity causes some men to break, others to break records." As a fifteen year old, I decided that I wanted to be that second breed of man.

Pros break records not just because they're skilled at what they do but because **they never allow adversity to break them.** Instead of fleeing from adversity, high performers welcome it as a worthy rival, and they rise to the level of their competition.

Adopting this mindset at an early age empowered me to take adversity head-on and use it as motivation. No matter where life took me, I vowed that I wouldn't let adversity prevent me from achieving the goals I had set for myself.

Reflection Questions

1. What does someone who embraces adversity look like to you? Describe this person. He or she could either be real or imagined.

2. Where will you eventually encounter adversity in pursuit of your goals?

PROS ARE CURIOUS

High performers are the most curious people you will ever meet. They are constantly looking for that one new idea that will give them an edge or a deeper understanding of an old concept that can help them take their game to a new level.

This applies not only to their profession or field of expertise but to anything they want to learn. By asking questions, reading books on their area of interest, and **relentlessly seeking new information,** pros are able to elevate their performance in *any* area where they choose to be great. They use an almost childlike curiosity as a true problem-solving skill and consistently outperform their peers and accelerate their growth with knowledge gained from others.

This, again, is what separates high performers from average performers. The average performer experiences some success and thinks he knows it all, while the high performer remains a dedicated student of his craft.

Reflection Questions

1. What kind of research could you do to better prepare yourself to achieve your goals?

2. Do you remember what it was like to be a child and curious about the world around you? What would it take to get back in touch with this part of yourself?

PROS SET GOALS

Goal setting is one of the most foundational principles of personal development and achievement. Knowing this, would it shock you to learn that, when surveyed, only 3% of the population stated they have clearly defined, written goals?

A Harvard Business study revealed that: 83% of the population does not have goals, 14% have a goal in mind, but not written down, and only 3% have specific, written goals. Further analysis of this study found that the 14% who have goals are ten times more successful than those without goals. The 3% with written goals are three times more successful than the 14% with unwritten goals. The science is clear on this, and while average performers can't be bothered to set, write down, or review their goals, true pros are busy doing all three, often on a daily basis.

Clearly defined goals provide clarity and focus, help you measure your progress, and keep you motivated when you might otherwise feel like giving up.

Don't make the mistake of overlooking this basic yet powerful habit. Set specific goals, write them down, review them daily, and put a plan in place to achieve them. Goal setting is a habit of nearly every high performer for one distinct reason: it works.

1. Do believe having a set of clearly defined, written goals is important? Why or why not?

2. What's a large, multi-step goal that you have right now? Write down the goal and the steps it will take to achieve that goal. Be as detailed as possible.

PROS INVEST IN THEMSELVES

Everyone has an excuse for why they aren't where they want to be. For many of us, it's a lack of time or money. We can't afford the right resources. But this excuse, like most excuses, stinks.

One of the first lessons I learned in the NFL was the importance of investing in your body. In that realm, this meant hiring a trainer, getting frequent massages, getting chiropractic treatment, and so forth—anything to assist your body in recovering and being able to perform at optimal levels. In the business world, this may mean investing in coaching, training, seminars, mentorship, or mastermind groups—anything that can help you do your job better and get better results.

Many high performers are known to be voracious readers and consumers of personal development material. Warren Buffet, Steve Jobs, and Ray Dalio are a few prime examples. **High performers know they are their best asset.** As such, they continuously pour into themselves to grow and be better.

If you think you don't have the time or money to afford the right resources, I encourage you to reevaluate and reprioritize. It's not an expense if you're investing in yourself.

Reflection Questions

1. How could you invest in yourself? What would it take (time, money, etc.), and how could you make it work?

2. What personal development books or courses have you been curious about? Write down a list of authors and topics that speak to you and your goals.

PROS SEEK CLARITY

One characteristic that's common among most high performers is their continuous desire for clarity.

High performers devote an inordinate amount of time to the practice of visualizing the future and determining what they want it to look like, sometimes down to the smallest detail. They ask themselves questions like:

- Who am I?
- Who do I want to be?
- What do I want?
- What do I value?
- In what areas do I excel?
- Where do I need to improve?

By asking and answering these questions, high achievers are able to clearly determine their current standing in the world and where they want to go moving forward.

It is almost impossible to plot a course to a particular destination if you haven't **clearly defined your destination** to begin with. More impossible still is breaking your journey down into actionable steps: knowing what you need to do, who you need to become, what skills you need to acquire, and what level of commitment, dedication, and courage will be required of you to complete your journey.

By first being clear about who they are and what they truly want, high performers are able to put a plan in place and then execute the plan with great precision.

Reflection Questions

1. Answer the questions in the bulleted list above in your notebook. Periodically return back to your list and write out new answers if your responses have changed.

2. What is your "destination"? Write out a vivid description of what you want your life to be like. What are your relationships like? What is your career, and what is going to work like? Where do you see yourself living and taking time to relax? Dream as big as you can here!

PROS EMBRACE CHANGE

While average performers are trying desperately to keep things the same, true pros know that change is inevitable, and they embrace it with all of their being.

Innovate or die; adapt or collapse. This is the mindset of a high performer, and it brings about a hunger for constant growth and evolution. Pros know that in an ever-changing world, **the secret is not to resist change but to confront it head-on** by learning new skills and embracing hew ways of thinking.

A pro comes at every new challenge with an upgraded operating system (mindset) and an attitude that change is good. Being open, adaptable, innovative, and flexible are the traits of a champion.

Reflection Questions

1. Think about a time when you resisted an inevitable change? How would your experience have been different if you embraced it?

2. What can you do to upgrade your mindset so that when challenges present themselves, you are ready?

PROS SUSPEND THEIR DISBELIEF

High performers are willing to look beyond something they consciously oppose and do it anyway. They may be convinced, deep down, that a particular strategy or tactic is *never* going to work, or they may not think a certain approach is the right one, but if the evidence suggests otherwise, they are willing to suspend their disbelief and have an open mind to give it a chance.

You already know how to temporarily suspend your disbelief. You do it anytime you watch the *Superman* or *Avengers* films. In order for you to enjoy that movie for those two hours, you just have to suspend your disbelief and accept what's happening on the screen. Even though you know consciously that people can't really fly or build high-tech superpowered suits, you allow yourself to temporarily ignore your own knowledge of the laws of physics in order to enjoy the movie. If you held firm to the limitations of being a human on Earth, you would sit through the whole movie being irritated, saying, "This is stupid. That wouldn't happen in real life. People can't fly. This is dumb." And *no one* wants to sit next to that guy.

There were a lot of times in my career when I had to suspend my own disbelief. In short, I had to keep an open mind. When I was with the 49ers, they coached us to always take an outside release on a "9" route. (If you're not familiar with these football terms, don't worry—the specifics don't matter here.)

Later, when I went to the Patriots, this habit had been so thoroughly drilled into me that I continued going outside anytime a "9" route was called. Finally, my coach asked me, "Why do you keep going outside? In that situation an inside release was better." He told me their philosophy was to take the best release based on the given situation. Initially, I thought, *No, that's wrong. If you have a crossing route coming, you don't want the defensive back to be able to look inside and possibly make a play on the crossing route.* But that wasn't my call. So even though I didn't necessarily agree with their philosophy, I had to be willing to say, "Okay, I don't think that's right, but I'll try it your way."

The point is, you may object to something initially. You may be tempted to dismiss a new strategy outright because, whether from personal experience or the guidance of a teacher along the way, you know different. But high performers are flexible. In fact, in my experience, the best performers I've ever been around were people who would say, **"I disagree with that, but let's try it and we'll see what happens."**

If you'll suspend your disbelief that something is not going to work—if you are willing to try it anyway—you might be surprised to find that a strategy you never considered before is actually incredibly powerful. This is about having an open mind, being willing to try new things, and having the humility to admit that you might not know it all. Even if you think you've got it all figured out, it's possible that there are other, better ways of doing things. Get out of your own way and be willing to explore alternative avenues toward achieving your goal.

Reflection Questions

1. In what areas of your life could you be more open-minded?

2. Recall and describe a situation where you didn't act with humility and you could have learned more if you had.

PROS HAVE SELF-DISCIPLINE

I think it almost goes without saying that self-discipline is one of the 33 Habits of All Pros. For any complex goal you take on, there are going to be things that you will have to do and to stop doing in order to succeed, all while pushing through any lack of motivation you might experience.

If you want to *start* getting up at 5:00 a.m. to work out, you'll have to *stop* staying up until 1:00 a.m. If you want to *start* that new side hustle you keep talking about, you'll have to *stop* wasting half your downtime playing video games. If you're going to lose 50 pounds, you not only need to *start* exercising, but you need to *stop* eating junk food, too.

There's just no way around it. You'll have to stop doing certain things if you want to start doing others. It's about **loving yourself enough to do what's best for you,** whether that's adding something to your life or removing something—or both. Self-discipline, therefore, exists on both ends of the spectrum, making it doubly important.

Reflection Questions

1. Name at least one thing you need to *start* doing to achieve your goals.

2. Name at least one thing you need to *stop* doing to achieve your goals.

PROS THINK BIG

When average performers are asked to define their goals or their vision—what they want most in life—they often tend to speak in terms of what they think is possible or what they think they can get. Their own self-doubt and limiting beliefs cause them to reduce the size and scope of their dreams to what they think is realistic. To be blunt, they play small and set the bar too low.

High performers have a deep belief that anything is possible and that human potential is limitless. The only questions in their minds are:

- What will it take?
- Am I willing to pay the price?

When JFK set his sights on going to the moon, he asked Werhner Von Braun what it would take to build a rocket that could carry a man to the moon and bring him back safely to Earth. Von Braun answered, "The will to do it." The question wasn't "Is it possible?" but rather, "What will it take?"

The mindset of thinking big allows high performers to set big goals and achieve things others think are impossible.

Reflection Questions

1. Write down your biggest, most outlandish goal. What will it take for you to reach that goal? Break it down into steps.

2. Are you willing to pay the price to achieve your biggest goal? Why or why not?

PROS PROGRAM THEMSELVES FOR SUCCESS

The process of self-examination forces a lot of people to wonder, *Why am I the way I am? Why do I feel, think, and act the way I do?* The answer to those questions is simple: mental programming.

Most of us received our current mental programming at an early age. It was "installed" by our parents, teachers, coaches, or authority figures. It is the foundation of our beliefs, thoughts, feelings, actions, and behaviors. Often, depending on the environment in which we grew up, the programming we received as kids is usually not sufficient to help us reach the high levels of success we desire as adults. High performers understand this and go the extra mile to devote themselves to the process of **reprogramming their outdated software.** They purge the thoughts and beliefs that no longer serve them and replace them by installing the habits, beliefs, traits, and characteristics of the champions they aspire to be.

Pros use two main methods to complete the programming process.

1. **Positive Self-Talk:** Bombarding the subconscious with positive affirmations—statements about the person you want to become and the success you desire—is the most powerful way to override and upgrade old programming.

2. **Visualization:** Positive mental images that depict your desired, ideal self—and the things you wish to do, have, and be—can have a tremendous effect on the way in which you experience the events in your life.

Positive Self-Talk

My thoughts on self-talk come from my background in neurolinguistic programming (NLP). The NLP perspective is essentially that the subconscious mind believes anything you tell it. So when you bombard your subconscious mind with self-talk such as "I'm so stupid," or "Things never work out for me," or "I'm not good enough at that," your subconscious will begin to believe those statements. You begin to believe these statements so firmly, in fact, that your subconscious mind then goes about the process of producing actions and behaviors that confirm that those statements are true. In other words, you will innately strive to prove yourself right about *whatever* you tell yourself—positive or negative.

In his book, *What to Say When You Talk to Yourself*, Shad Helmstetter describes the concept of 148,000 nos:

> *During the first eighteen years of our lives, if we grew up in fairly average, reasonably positive homes, we were told "No!" or what we could not do, or what would not work, more than 148,000 times. If you were more fortunate, you may have been told "No" only 100,000 times, or 50,000 times—however many, it was considerably more negative programming than any of us needs.*

In a world where we spend so much time talking negatively to ourselves, positive self-talk is a game-changer. This isn't just about confidence. Your subconscious mind believes that what you say about yourself must be true and will go about the process of making that the reality. Armed with this knowledge, positive self-talk—from an athlete's perspective—can include phrases such as "I am great," "I always perform under pressure," "I make every catch," and "I run my routes with precision."

This is where so many athletes get their confidence from: the combination of physical repetition and that bombardment on the subconscious of positive, affirming statements. It's not that they're egomaniacs—although, I'll admit, some of them might be. It's that they're programming themselves for success.

You will increase the likelihood of your success when you realize that your behaviors and actions will naturally manifest in physical form to match the deeply held beliefs you have about yourself. For example, throughout my entire career in the NFL, I never had confidence issues about catching the ball because my self-talk was centered around phrases such as "I catch *every* ball I can get my hands on."

What we say to ourselves matters, and the most successful people I have been around were much more inclined to speak positively to themselves.

Visualization

Several years ago, I came across a University of Chicago study aimed at determining the power of visualization. In the study, Dr. Judd Biasiotto, a sports psychologist, split a group of undergraduate students into three groups. All three groups shot free throws to establish a baseline free-throw percentage. Over the course of the next month, the first group practiced shooting free throws every day. The second group only practiced visualizing shooting free throws with perfect form and making every shot. This group was instructed to visualize, in great detail, the form, seeing the ball go in the net, and successfully making every shot. The third group did nothing—no practice and no visualization.

At the end of the month, all three groups were tested again to gauge their improvement. The group that had spent their time actually shooting and practicing the free throws had a 24 percent improvement. The group that didn't practice at all, and instead only visualized, had a 23 percent improvement. The group that had done nothing showed no improvement.

I find this study fascinating because it proves the incredible power of visualization. It's no surprise that the group who spent that time physically practicing showed the highest degree of improvement. And it's no surprise that the third group didn't improve at all. But isn't it amazing that the second group—just by visualizing making free throws without performing the physical motions—improved to a degree that nearly matched the group that practiced? It's positive proof that your brain interprets thoughts as reality; through visualization, you make real neurological connections that can improve your performance *without* even physically doing the thing. Just by visualizing yourself performing the way you want to perform, an observable, quantifiable improvement is possible.

These two techniques, positive self-talk and visualization, are simple yet extremely powerful tools to add to your success arsenal.

Reflection Questions

1. Create five positive self-talk statements that will make a difference in one area of your life.

2. Visualize your ideal self. What do you look like? What are you wearing? What do you have? Write down what you visualized and return to this image regularly.

PROS KEEP THINGS IN PERSPECTIVE

Is one hundred dollars a lot of money? The correct way to answer this question is with another question: Compared to what?

Big and small are relative terms, and almost everything in life depends on what you are comparing it to. Many of us are raised to think objectively, but a subjective mentality is a more beneficial long-term strategy. Compared to *one* dollar—yes, one hundred dollars is a lot of money! But compared to a *million* dollars, it's not much at all. This may seem like a useless distinction, but **high performers are masters at using perspective to their advantage.**

I like to give the example of Michael Jordan's gambling habits. Michael loved to gamble. He would gamble on anything and everything—rounds of golf with friends, games of skill with arena security, poker with teammates on the plane the next city. It didn't matter if it was big or small money. It was a way for Jordan to relieve stress.

Much was made about Jordan's gambling habits off the field, and he became frustrated with all the focus the press placed on his gambling. He was, after all, placing wagers mostly on himself—betting on his own performance. When asked if he had a gambling problem, Michael replied, "I have a competition problem."

When it came out that Jordan had written a $57,000 check to Slim Bouler to cover a wager, eyebrows began to raise. Soon after that, a golfing acquaintance, Richard Esquinas, claimed that Jordan owed him $1.2 million in gambling debts. The media went wild. Suddenly, there was rampant speculation about Jordan's integrity. But here's where perspective is key. In the docuseries *The Last Dance*, former NBA Commissioner David Stern told filmmakers, "It never reached epic crisis levels in my view." And what he said next really hammered the point home: "You have to understand that $57,000 is not a lot of money to Michael Jordan. He was the world's highest-paid athlete in 1992. His salary was $4 million a year in the early 90s with an estimated $32 million from product endorsements in 1992 alone."

People were reacting to Michael's gambling debts based on their own context. Considering that the average household income in 1992 was $22,000, you can bet that a $57,000 check seemed like a lot of money to the general public. And anyone with $1.2 million in gambling debts *must* have a gambling problem! But we're not talking about *anyone*. We're talking about Michael Jordan. For the world's highest-paid athlete, that sort of debt was entirely manageable.

Pros think subjectively. They measure the tradeoff of cost versus reward in terms of perspective. The commitment of resources that may be required of you *now* to work on your craft might seem like a lot, but when measured against the payoff that awaits you in the future, it's a drop in the bucket.

Reflection Questions

1. Can you think of a time when black-and-white thinking may have unintentionally hindered your progress?

2. What is the potential cost of pursuing a long-term goal that you have? What does the payoff look like?

HABIT 15:

PROS TAKE RISKS

Average performers have been conditioned to play it safe and to avoid risk at all costs. This strategy of risk aversion is fine...if you want to be average.

High performers know that **without risk, there is little progress and certainly no reward.** Yes, there is the possibility of loss, but pros have such unwavering belief in themselves that they know they can get back anything they lose.

Every Hail Mary pass has the chance of being a colossal blunder instead of the exclamation point on a victory. Every player who attempts a buzzer-beating three-pointer runs the risk of becoming the game-losing pariah instead of their city's hero. Pros are willing to take that risk and live with the consequences, good or bad.

As the great Wayne Gretzky said, "You miss 100 percent of the shots you don't take." While that statement is almost cliché these days, nothing could be truer. If the goal is to arrive safely at death, stay in your comfort zone, but if you wish to push the limits and test yourself, you have to take risks.

In the story I shared earlier, the Barnyard Forty, I took a risk racing a horse. But the reward, $500 for a broke college kid, was worth the gamble. I believed in myself and my abilities, and I was willing to live with the consequences if I didn't succeed.

Reflection Questions

1. What fear is holding you back from taking more risks in your life?

2. What is one risk you could take right now that could pay off massively in your life?

PROS ARE BOLD

High performers are masters of creating and manifesting their vision through boldness. While average performers are waiting for permission to be great, true pros know that greatness is there for the taking if they are courageous and bold enough to grab it.

When it comes to achieving their goals, pros understand that there is no need to be liked, accepted, or approved of. High performers **focus only on what is necessary to get the desired outcome** and know how to do it with class and integrity. What average performers see as pushy or overly aggressive, pros see as simply a necessary part of the process to be their best and accomplish the mission.

Michael Jordan and Kobe Bryant were both notorious for *not* being well liked by competitors—or even by their teammates, at times. Michael has been described as a downright bully during practice because of his high intensity, and Kobe was relentless about holding his teammates to the same high standards he set for himself. The idea of being liked and respected by one's peers is not the primary focus of high performers, as nice as that might be. Michael and Kobe may not have been well liked, but everyone loved the championships they delivered for their organizations, teams, and cities.

Be bold, and be great.

Reflection Questions

1. Who is one person you admire that has the trait of boldness?

2. Do you consider yourself a bold person? If not, how can you work to become bolder in your day-to-day life?

PROS HAVE HIGH EXPECTATIONS

Champions don't hope to win. They expect to win.

While amateurs believe that high expectations will lead to disappointment, **a pro's expectation is never anything less than the most desirable outcome.**

Every single super-high performer I have met has believed they would come out on top and get the desired outcome, even when the odds were against them. Do *you* believe you can upgrade your results simply by upgrading your expectations? Champions do, and they use this mental trick to their advantage.

I've used this habit countless times in my life and career, with great success. By programming your mind through positive self-talk and visualization to always expect the best, your subconscious goes about the process of creating the actions and behaviors necessary to produce that desired outcome.

Amateurs have low expectations and hope for the best. Pros know the outcome is up to them, and they *expect* to win.

Reflection Questions

1. In what areas of your life could you expect better for yourself?

2. Do you have a mindset that says: "High expectations lead to disappointment"? If so, can you pinpoint an experience or set of experiences that led to this mindset?

PROS ARE DEDICATED

While amateurs say they want to accomplish something and then give up at the first sign of adversity or struggle, pros set their sights on a target and stay dedicated to the process, no matter what.

To the dedicated pro, roadblocks, obstacles, or bumps in the road are used as steppingstones on the path to achieving the desired outcome. No amount of pain, exhaustion, setbacks, or disappointment can knock them off track. If they don't have the answer, they find it. If they don't currently have the skills necessary, they work to acquire them. If they don't have the resources, they find people who can help.

True dedication is borne of passion, commitment, desire, self-discipline, and inspiration. Pros combine these elements to create a mindset that says *if I can't go over it or around it, I'll go through it*. Their dedication to achieving the desired outcome is what sets them apart from average performers and propels them to consistently succeed and excel, while others give up.

Reflection Questions

1. Think back to a time you set a goal that you didn't achieve. Were you as dedicated as you could have been? If not, why?

2. What's one area of your life or career you can be more dedicated to? How will that area improve once you are more dedicated?

PROS TAKE ACTION

One of my college coaches once told a story about two frogs sitting on a lily pad. "One of the frogs decided he wanted to jump into the pond," said the coach. "How many frogs are left on the lily pad?"

"One!" everyone yelled.

Coach smiled, then joyfully corrected us. "No," he said, "there's still two frogs on the lily pad. Just because he *decided* to jump doesn't mean he did."

Coach's parable was a rather silly way to make an important point—simply deciding to do something won't get the thing done. While average performers take the necessary steps of making plans and deciding what needs to be done, they often stop there and fall short of the high performers who are busy taking action.

Pros are notorious dreamers and bold visionaries, but it's their **willingness to take action and execute** that sets them apart. Many great ideas have never come to fruition due to a lack of action or initiative. In between sketching the blueprint of your dream house and living in it is the action you must take to actually build it.

Reflection Questions

1. What's a vision that you have had that has yet to come to fruition?

2. What kind of person do you need to become in order to bring your vision to life?

PROS ARE COURAGEOUS

We like to think of *fearlessness* and *courage* as synonymous, but I disagree. I believe there is no courage absent of some type of fear. So my thought on courage is simple. Courage is when you are fearful and you go for it anyway.

Every high performer has broken through a barrier where that element of fear was present. They all know what it means to question themselves and wonder, *Is this really the right thing to do? Am I on the right path?*

Even the most highly skilled individuals face this fear, especially given that there are so many easier, safer paths to take in life. We all have that animal instinct inside us, telling us to run and hide—to flee from what's difficult in favor of comfort and ease. There's a constant internal dialogue, in the guise of self-preservation, telling us to seek safety and shelter.

I remember having that conversation with myself every time I lined up to run down and cover a kickoff. I would say a little prayer, "Lord, protect me! This is going to be high-speed, high-impact, and anything can happen." In some ways, I was afraid, but I went anyway. A first-time entrepreneur faces this same situation when they decide to take the risk and finally start that business. It's a scary prospect, and there are a million legitimate reasons not to do it. But on the other side of that fear is everything they want. So they do it despite their fear.

Acting in spite of fear has many applications beyond your career. A lot of times, it's about speaking up for what you think is right. Standing up against an injustice means stepping outside your comfort zone, but you do it anyway because you know it's right. For example, you might be fearful of the repercussions of taking a certain stance on social issues or racial inequality. But you do it anyway. Because the change is worth it.

Likewise, high levels of success or achievement are going to require you to **live outside your comfort zone.** That means having the courage to strike out and follow a dream—to tell everyone you know that *this* is what you want to do. You cannot move forward if your fear of stepping into something new or taking a risk debilitates you. Feeling that fear and taking action in spite of it is a trademark characteristic of high performers and successful people.

Reflection Questions

1. When did fear prevent you from doing something you really wanted to do or standing up for what was right?

2. What is a cause that you could take action for right now?

HABIT 21:

PROS OVERCOME THE FEAR OF OTHER PEOPLE'S OPINIONS

The vast majority of society is dependent on the approval of others. So much so that the fear of being rejected, ridiculed, or laughed at hamstrings many of us right out of the gate. This has always been the case to some degree, for average performers, but things have gotten even worse with the rise of social media. Some of us are actually *addicted* to others' approval or validation, experiencing depressive-like symptoms when we don't get enough likes on a social media photo or post and experiencing a quick dopamine rush when we get likes, comments, and engagement with something we put out there.

But the road to greatness is littered with the corpses of those who have let the opinions of others prevent them from expressing their true selves and going all out for the things they want in life. But high performers know that **ridicule comes with the territory.** Most of the cheap shots come from the people sitting in the stands—hecklers and naysayers watching the pro lay it on the line and operate in their gift.

Kobe Bryant claimed that his ability to ignore the boos came from his conscious decision to ignore the cheers, too; validating the positive feedback would have meant that he had to recognize the negative feedback as being equally credible. To prevent this, he chose to disregard praise and criticism alike. In the minds of high performers, the only opinions that matter are their own, and those of the select few coaches, mentors, and advisors they have trusted to be in their inner circle.

Reflection Questions:

1. In what areas of life do you seek approval from others?

2. What positive results might come into your life if you were able to disregard others' opinions?

PROS TAKE RESPONSIBILITY

True pros never play the blame game. While amateurs are looking for excuses for why they didn't get it done, pros are already looking in the mirror for the answers.

Nearly every high performer I have ever been around takes the following position: "**I am the problem, and I am the solution.** When I get better, my results will improve." They know they are completely responsible for their successes *and* failures, and they wouldn't have it any other way.

Putting yourself on the *cause* side of the cause/effect equation empowers you to make the changes necessary to get the desired outcome, rather than living with a victim mentality, hopeless to change to the situation.

Reflection Questions:

1. Think back to a time when someone you knew or spoke to was clearly embracing a victim mentality. How did that make you feel about them?

2. In what areas of your life do you feel like the victim? What would change about this area of your life if you put yourself on the "cause" side of the cause/effect equation?

PROS ARE COACHABLE

The ability to learn new things is a trait present in all high performers, but what sets true pros apart is the ability to implement and apply what they've learned. This is the key distinction between being teachable and being coachable.

Being teachable means you're capable of learning something, but being coachable means you're willing and able to actually do it—to **submit to the process and execute.** Most people are teachable. They're willing to learn something new. But they aren't always willing to put what they've learned into practice.

I played for several different teams in my NFL career. Every team had a different way of doing some of the most basic things, and they expected their players to do these things the way *they* wanted them done...regardless of how a particular player may have learned to do something in the past or with a previous team.

Players who are not coachable don't stick around very long in the NFL. I made the decision early in my career that I would be *coachable*. I would do what I was being asked to do, the way I was being asked to do it. This choice undoubtedly added years to my career.

Reflection Questions

1. Would you say that you are coachable? Why or why not?

2. What is one area of your life where you would benefit from being more coachable?

PROS SURROUND THEMSELVES WITH GREATNESS

Jim Rohn famously said that you become the average of the five people you spend the most time around. If there's any truth to this statement, then it stands to reason that it's incredibly important to **be aware and deliberate about who you choose to spend time with.**

One of my mentors used to say that consciousness is contagious. The quickest way to get better, dream bigger, and achieve more is to intentionally interact with people who are better than you, have bigger goals and dreams than you, and are high achievers. You will grow and evolve just by being around these people and by listening to their conversations, seeing things from their perspective, and observing the way they go about their work.

Reflection Questions

1. Can you recall a time when someone you were close to kept you from reaching your goals in a certain area? Describe the situation and your current reflections. What could you have done differently?

2. Write down some places where you could meet people who could elevate you.

PROS PRACTICE GRATITUDE

Ancient philosophers believed that gratitude was a foundational human emotion and that, when cultivated, it could enhance well-being, deepen relationships, improve optimism, and increase happiness.

I strongly believe that no one succeeds alone or strictly of their own doing. Acknowledging this through the practice of deliberate, habitual gratitude will go a long way toward achieving the results predicted by the philosophers above.

Practicing gratitude or appreciation for the people and things in your life—essential factors that have contributed to making you who and what you are—is essential. High performers make **practicing gratitude a habit of their daily lives,** and they reap the benefits.

Reflection Questions

1. Write a thank-you letter to someone who has helped you get to where you are today. Send this person your letter or give them a call to express your appreciation.

2. How can you make gratitude a part of your daily life? Brainstorm some ideas here.

PROS PAY THE PRICE

Average performers are often shocked to discover the amount of time, energy, and sacrifice that true pros expend to reach the level of success they have attained. Most people find it easier on their own egos to believe that pros are endowed with some innate, superhuman talent. Or maybe they just got lucky! Or maybe every high performer out there is someone who found a "hack" or a shortcut to accelerate their progress. We *want* to believe this because it would mean that greatness was attainable *without* hard work, if only we could unlock the "secret." But the truth is, all pros know that **there is no shortcut; there is only sacrifice**, and they gladly pay the price.

High performers understand the concept of delayed gratification. They gladly endure the blood, sweat, and tears *now* for the payoff later.

While others are relaxing at the beach or celebrating moderate levels of success, the pro is putting in the work. This is the true driver of greatness. Pay the price *now* so you can live the life you want later.

Reflection Questions

1. Reflect on a time when you could have delayed gratification in pursuit of a bigger goal.

2. What is one sacrifice you could make now to put you in a better situation (in your health, relationships, finances, career, etc.)?

PROS ARE PERSISTENT

When asked for a list of "keys to success," nearly every high performer will note the quality of persistence near the top of their list, if not at position number one.

The will to get back up after being knocked down, and then keep moving forward—this is a staple of any champion. Amateurs tend to give up at the first sign of adversity or failure, but true pros know that **adversity and failure are opportunities to learn, grow, and come back stronger.**

Can you imagine if a child decided to give up walking after numerous failed attempts? What if every baby who fell down decided that walking was too hard—that anything but crawling simply couldn't be done?

Rarely do we get things right the first time. Through persistence, nearly any mountain can be climbed and any challenge overcome.

I was cut seven times in my NFL career. Technically, I *failed* seven times to reach my goal or realize "success." But I got back up every time and kept moving forward. I never allowed those failures to defeat me or cause me to give up on the dream. I encourage you—no, I *challenge* you—to do the same. Failure is an opportunity to learn, grow, and get better. You *will* get another shot. And if you stay persistent, you'll be prepared when that second, third, or sixth chance comes knocking at your door.

Reflection Questions

1. Describe a time in your life that you gave up too early. How do you think things could have turned out differently if you showed more persistence?

2. What is one area of your life where you could show more persistence to get what you want?

PROS COMPARTMENTALIZE

I can't begin to count the number of times I've heard someone utter some variation of the following sentence: "I was putting in the work and making great progress, but then... (fill in the blank)." Sometimes it's, "things got crazy at work." Or, "I had some family drama going on at home." Or, "I was under a lot of stress." Bottom line, amateurs have a tendency to allow a problem in one area of life or business to affect other unrelated pursuits. This inability to compartmentalize or separate the facets of their life causes them to get bogged down and decreases performance on the task at hand.

A trait present in all high performers is the ability to **handle multiple issues without becoming overwhelmed.** Professional athletes are masters at being able to "lock in" when it's game time. This is to say, the outside world, their personal problems, or whatever else may have been on their mind, gets locked away—stored in a separate room or "compartment" while they go about doing their job with full focus and attention on the current task at hand.

One of the exercises I often have my clients perform to improve their ability to compartmentalize is to "walk the hallway." Imagine you are walking down a long hallway with many doors on each side. Inside each room are the different "problems" you may be dealing with or tasks you need to complete at any given time. Let's say, for example, you need to lock in on a big project at work. As you enter that room and close the door behind you, you shut off all the noise and distractions—which are safely locked away in their respective rooms along the hallway. With the door shut, these other problems are unable to affect you or interrupt your work on the task at hand. When you finish with that task, you exit that room, enter the next room that needs your attention, and repeat the process. The idea is to train your mind to focus on one problem or task at a time. When you are at work, your mind is at work. When you're home with your family, your focus is on them. When it's game time, your personal life is locked away in another room, unable to distract or divert your focus from the task at hand.

Reflection Questions

1. Have you ever found yourself getting stressed out at work when something happened to you in a relationship? Describe the situation and how you could have changed the course of your day by compartmentalizing.

2. Have you ever reacted negatively to a loved one due to a stressful life event? How did it make the other person feel? How did it impact your relationship with this person?

PROS SIMPLIFY

Average performers have convinced themselves that success is a complex process. It just can't be as simple as adopting a few new habits and implementing several key ideas that have been proven over time. But high performers know that the opposite is true. Pros make the complicated simple.

If you want to lose weight and be healthier, eat less junk and exercise more.

If you want to improve your business, increase your sales and/ or profit margin and reduce your costs.

If you don't know how, learn.

Every offseason as an NFL player, I would identify one thing I wanted to be better at in the following season. My training program was then centered around improving in this area while continuing to strengthen the areas I was already good at. **Simplifying the process down to a few key concepts** and executing on them is the practice of high performers.

Reflection Questions

1. What is one time that you have overcomplicated an issue in your life?

2. Think about the following areas of your life: health, relationships, career, and personal development. Write down a simple statement about what you can do to improve each area.

HABIT 30:

PROS STOP COMPETING

We've all heard the saying that the man or woman in the mirror is your only competition.

Guess what? It's true.

I lived the majority of my life in extremely competitive environments. I was always trying to be better than my competition. And, in the short term, this was a good thing. It kept me in a mindset of constant improvement. The thought that someone else was working out and strategizing to be better than me got me out of bed in the morning. It provided the motivation necessary for me to give my best, day in and day out. But, over time, the desire to be better than someone else faded, and I realized that the greatest motivator was simply the desire to be *my* best self.

Pros understand that **manifesting the best version of yourself** is what allows you to become and remain consistently great. This makes success a never-ending journey.

After Michael Jordan won three NBA championships and was universally recognized as the greatest basketball player of all time, what was his motivation to win three *more*? Simple: He wanted to see just how great he could be—how much higher he could take his game. He wasn't interested in what anyone else was doing, only what *he* could create and how much greater *he* could become.

If success was just about competing, then winning would be the end of the story. But winning is just the start of the next season.

This subtle shift in mindset is what allows high performers to stay motivated and be consistently great, while others plateau.

Reflection Questions

1. What is one area of your life where you could make consistent gains and track your progress?

2. Do you like competing with others? Why or why not? If you are a competitive person, how could you apply the satisfaction competition brings to your relationship with yourself?

PROS ARE COMEBACK ARTISTS

Ask any of the world's most successful people how many times they have failed—and failed miserably—and their answer will be "countless."

We have all heard the story of Steve Jobs being fired from Apple, the company he founded in his garage, only to return and build Apple into one the greatest, most impactful companies of our time. And did you know that Abraham Lincoln lost eight elections before being elected president? What if he had given up after his first failed attempt?

As spectators, we see the successes of high performers; we don't always see that those successes came only after bouncing back from multiple failures. The pro's ability to persevere and continue getting up after getting knocked down is what separates them from their peers.

True pros simply don't understand what it means to give up. They are willing to persevere at all costs. Their never-say-die attitudes cause them to believe that setbacks are setups for comebacks.

Reflection Questions

1. What is one goal or dream you've given up on where you could possibly make a comeback?

PROS ARE CONSISTENT

One of the hallmarks of a true pro is the ability to perform at the highest levels, consistently. Anyone can be great once. But what separates elite level performers from the rest of the pack is their ability to be great day in and day out—on the big things and small things, alike.

During my time with the New England Patriots, head coach Bill Belichick used the phrase "string them together" when speaking about consistency.

One day after practice, he approached me and said, "You had a great practice yesterday and another great one today. Come out tomorrow, have another great practice, and just keep stringing them together."

Love them or hate them, the Patriots' greatness cannot be questioned—winning seventeen AFC East Division Championships, nine AFC Conference Championships, and six Super Bowls in the span of Belichick's twenty-plus years as head coach.

That level of greatness can only be achieved by taking consistent, daily action around the habits, practices, and the big things and the small things alike.

Reflection Questions

1. What is one area of your life where you could be more consistent in your approach to success?

2. How does consistency (in the way you are treated in relationships, at work, etc.) lead to healthier and more productive results in your life? How do you respond when someone behaves inconsistently or expectations at work are inconsistent?

PROS LIVE TO GIVE

The belief that life is about what you give, not what you get, is one of the hallmarks of a true champion.

High performers live with an abundance mindset. They understand that there's enough to go around for everyone. While average performers live with an "I'll do this for you if you do this for me" mindset, pros know that **the secret is to give and ask nothing in return**—the opposite of the amateur's transactional, quid-pro-quo mindset.

It's not necessarily that high performers are more generous; it's that they know that the reservoir is infinitely deep. The source will never run dry. While many people believe you have to give in order to get, true pros focus on just giving and, in turn, receive more and attract more due to their abundance-based mindset.

Reflection Questions:

1. Write about a time when you did something only to receive something in return.

2. How could you freely give more of yourself in your day-to-day life? What is something you could start doing today?

THE 33 HABITS OF ALL PROS

Here, again, are the 33 habits you can implement in your life to Be a Pro.

Habit 1: Pros Have World-Class Habits

Habit 2: Pros Are Honest

Habit 3: Pros Are Decisive

Habit 4: Pros Welcome Adversity

Habit 5: Pros Are Curious

Habit 6: Pros Set Goals

Habit 7: Pros Invest in Themselves

Habit 8: Pros Seek Clarity

Habit 9: Pros Embrace Change

Habit 10: Pros Suspend Their Disbelief

Habit 11: Pros Have Self-Discipline

Habit 12: Pros Think Big

Habit 13: Pros Program Themselves for Success

Habit 14: Pros Keep Things in Perspective

Habit 15: Pros Take Risks

Habit 16: Pros Are Bold

Habit 17: Pros Have High Expectations

Habit 18: Pros Are Dedicated

Habit 19: Pros Take Action

Habit 20: Pros Are Courageous

Habit 21: Pros Overcome the Fear of Other People's Opinions

CONCLUSION

If this book helps you get better, achieve a goal or dream, make more money, take your career to the next level, have more of the things you want, and become the best version of yourself, then I'm absolutely thrilled for you! But if all I've achieved up to this point was to help you *get* more and be more successful, then I've failed you. I've missed the mark of what I truly want to communicate. So, I want to take these last few pages and tell you why this *really* matters...why it's so important that you create the best version of yourself and be a pro.

Getting more and having more is great. Don't get me wrong; success is a worthy pursuit. From an early age, it's been drilled into our psyches that success is the metric we should measure ourselves against. I spent nearly all of my teens and twenties in the pursuit of success. And I caught it. I achieved my goal of playing in the NFL. It was great, and I loved every second of it. I won a Super Bowl, made several million dollars before my thirtieth birthday, and lived my dream. I was a success. But here's the kicker: it wasn't enough.

How many people do you know who have said something similar? Maybe you've said it yourself. After getting everything you ever wanted—money, success, material possessions—deep down, you were not fulfilled.

Is that it? Is this all there is? When I retired from the NFL and began to reflect on my life and what I had accomplished up to that point, those questions nagged me...constantly. As I was searching for the answers, several more questions around my "success" began to surface: Who or what did it serve? Who benefitted? Who was better off because of what I had accomplished? The answer to those questions was obvious, and singular: me.

Sure, I was able to help my family, donate to various charities, and use my platform as a pro athlete to do some good in the community, but the overwhelming benefactor of my success was still me.

And while I didn't feel selfish or guilty for pursing a passion and achieving a lifelong dream, I knew in that moment that I no longer wanted to pursue success. Personal success wasn't, and never would be, enough. I wanted something deeper, more fulfilling, and more purposeful: Significance.

Significance can be summed up in three words: impact, influence, and contribution. While success asks, "What can I get?", significance asks, "What can I give?" I believe Winston Churchill said it best: "You make a living by what you get. You make a life by what you give." At our core, human beings are driven by a desire to contribute. When asked, most people will identify moments they gave to someone in need, contributed to something bigger than themselves, or made a positive impact in someone's life as the things that brought them the greatest sense of fulfillment.

I know you agree. You've no doubt experienced this in your own life. You know what it feels like to be significant—impactful, influential, and making meaningful contributions to your loved ones, and society as whole.

I got my first real taste of significance in 2004 when I started my own nonprofit organization, the Jimmy Farris Future Leaders

Foundation. My goal was to cultivate leadership skills in youth—particularly underprivileged youth—in the greater Atlanta community where I was living at the time, as well as my hometown of Lewiston, Idaho.

One of the first events we did was a football camp in Lewiston. I brought several of my teammates back to Lewiston and held the camp at the Boys and Girls Club. It was a chance for the kids to interact with real-life NFL players and an opportunity for us to really pour into them. It was a great day for everyone.

Anytime you do an event like that, there is a price tag. At the time, I had done one fundraiser and had roughly $6,000 in my foundation account. When the Falcons heard I was doing the camp, Falcons owner Arthur Blank sent me a nice note congratulating me and expressing his excitement over what we were doing. One of the problems with doing the camp in Idaho, however, was that I needed to fly everyone who was involved with the camp into Lewiston, which is not the easiest place in the world to get to. I knew it was going to be expensive, so I asked Mr. Blank if he would charter his plane for us to bring everybody to Idaho. He politely declined—and I don't blame him—so I bit the bullet and spent nearly $5,000 for plane tickets.

The camp was a hit. The kids had a great time and benefited from the teaching on and off the field. The community really came together and supported the cause, and I was extremely proud of my hometown! My teammates and the group of people I brought with me also had an unbelievable experience. I learned so much from that first camp and identified a lot that we could do better the next time around. We hadn't budgeted things very well, and many last-minute issues came up that cost me a good deal of money. I ended up writing a check for close to $7,500 out of my personal bank account to cover the expenses.

When I got back to training camp in August, Mr. Blank approached me on the practice field and asked me how the camp had gone. I told him it was a great experience for everybody involved, and I related some of what I had learned about how to make it better the next time around. I also shared that we hadn't budgeted very well and that I'd ended up spending about $7,500 of my own money. His response was interesting.

Rather than sympathize with me or offer some advice about how I could do it better next time, Mr. Blank simply said, "Good. You spent some money paying it forward to the community that raised you. That's always a good investment."

It wasn't until years later, reflecting on that moment, that I fully understood what Mr. Blank was referring to. Impact. Influence. Contribution. *Significance.*

And that's what I'm referring to here. That's what this book is truly about. That's why I believe it's so important that you create the best version of yourself and become a true pro, so that you are *able* to be more impactful, influential, and contribute even more to the people you love, and to the world. So that every person you come in contact with benefits from you and is positively impacted in some way.

There's an old story that sometimes makes its way around NFL facilities. It's a story about a player named Able. Throughout my career, several of my coaches told this story.

Able possessed all the qualities every coach would want in a player. Able was depend<u>able</u>, reli<u>able</u>, adapt<u>able</u>, cap<u>able</u>, teach<u>able</u>, coach<u>able</u>, account<u>able</u>, and most importantly, avail<u>able</u>.

"Every player should strive to be just like Able," my coaches said. "He could do it all. He was an *impact* player."

Able: having the power, skill, means, or opportunity to do something.

There is a reason why flights attendants instruct you to put on your oxygen mask before assisting others. It's the same reason it's so important for you to be your best and to become the best version of yourself: So you are *able* to be impactful, to contribute, and to help others in their time of need. Your family, loved ones, and anyone else you are fortunate to touch need your very best. They deserve your "A" game. The world needs you...the *best* version of you.

With that in mind, now it's time for your final Reflection Questions.

Reflection Questions

1. How am I impacting other people?

2. Are people better because they've come in contact with me?

3. How can I be more significant in the lives my loved ones, friends, colleagues, and the world?

ACKNOWLEDGEMENTS

The process of writing this book caused me to reach deep into the memories of my past. Almost daily, many of the experiences, stories, and people—some I hadn't thought about in years—suddenly popped into the forefront of mind, causing me to laugh, cry, and wonder why I've been so fortunate to have been touched and impacted by so many amazing individuals and life experiences. I firmly believe that no one succeeds alone. We all need people in our corner supporting us, investing in us, going to bat to for us, and giving us opportunities. My life is a testament to this. At every turn, I've been blessed to encounter people who went above and beyond to contribute to my life and success.

Nothing I've accomplished in life would be possible without the love, support, and encouragement of my family—my parents, Bob and Sharon; my siblings, Mike, Lainey, Jaime, and Dave; my sister-in-law, Sam; my brothers-in-law, Brian and Matt; my nephews, Joe, Jake, Cooper, Blake, Sam, Cade, and Terry; and my niece, Sydni. All of you have impacted my life immensely and given me more love and support than I deserve.

To my best and lifelong friends, Billy, Karon "K-boogie," Jeremy "Son," Raychel, Justin, Chanler, Shawn "The Springs," Alma, and Tank. You have either been there from the very beginning or came into my life by divine appointment, just when I needed you most. Thank you for the contributions you've made in my life. I am better and my life is richer because of each one of you. I can only hope I've been as meaningful to you and your journey as you've been to mine. I love you all dearly.

To my first coach, Nick Menegas. Where do I begin? My football career would never have happened without you and your influence. Meeting you at the age of nine, as a fourth grader, on the practice fields at Lewiston High School, was the beginning of a journey that allowed me to live a dream. Your guidance, mentorship, love, and unwavering support of me, and all that I've accomplished or attempted, has touched me in ways I could never fully express. Thank you, Coach. Love you, man.

To Coach George Stewart. Big George. Big Stew. "Be A Pro" belongs to you. You say it, live it, embody it, and encourage it in everyone you meet. I've said countless times, to anyone who would listen, beginning my NFL career with the 49ers and having you as my coach was the difference between me being a guy who got a chance but never made it and me having a six-year career and being a Super Bowl Champion. I could never quantify the impact you've made on me as a player, and more importantly as a man. Thank you.

To Joe Gibbs, you gave me an opportunity to be a part of an amazing team and an historic franchise. But more than that, you *believed in me.* You went to bat for me and chose me when there were other options available. Playing for you and being able to call you my coach is one of the highlights of my NFL career. Thank you for being the coach and the man that you are. You are an example to all of what it truly means to be significant.

To Isaac Stegman, thank you for believing in me, investing in me, supporting me, and encouraging me. This book and my career in this industry would not have been possible without you. You brought me into your world and gave me a chance when I needed it the most. I'm forever grateful.

To Matt McGillivray, Beth Walker, and Blair Anderson, thank you for believing in me and trusting me. Regardless of where this career and project take me, you guys will always represent the "beginning" and will forever be "founding members."

To Kevin Van Valkenburg. From Aber Hall, to Briggs St., and beyond, your consummate friendship and support and guidance in all of my writing endeavors is so greatly appreciated. Your talent and brilliance continue to amaze me. I'm proud of you and thankful for the many contributions you've made in my life.

To Karen Rowe and her team at Front Rowe Seat. Thank you for your hard work in getting this project this started. Your vision, patience, and expertise are the reason these thoughts and ideas got out of my head and onto paper.

To Jessie Krieger, Zora Knauf, and the entire team at Lifestyle Entrepreneurs Press, thank you for believing in me and this project. Writing and publishing a book has been a goal of mine for 20 years. You all helped me realize that goal and bring this book to life. I am proud of what we created, together. More to come.

To all of my friends, former coaches (Nilsson, Cornelia, Richel, Cockhill, Pease, Dennehy, Joe Glenn, Mooch, Knapper, Belichick, Dan Reeves, Jim Mora, Joe D, Danny Smith), and acquaintances who have touched me, supported me, believed in me, encouraged me, impacted my life, or contributed in some way, big or small, thank you! From the bottom of my heart, thank you. This book is the cumulation of all the experiences, lessons, conversations, laughs, tears, and moments we've shared at one time or another. All of you contributed to this project greatly. There are pieces of you in the greater story of my life, and in every page of this book.